THE LOST PLEASURES OF THE
GREAT TRAINS

THE LOST PLEASURES OF THE
GREAT TRAINS

Martin Page

William Morrow and Company, Inc.

New York

Printed in England.

Library of Congress Catalog Card Number 75-13623

ISBN 0-688-02951-5

Contents

For James Page and his grandparents

A Single to St Petersburg

Recently Sir John Betjeman, the Poet Laureate, nostalgically possessed as so many others have been by the aged and soot-covered but still discernible destination signs outside Blackfriars Station in London, went to the booking office and requested a ticket to St Petersburg. The clerk, apparently as unaffected by the course of modern history as the sign, helpfully referred him to Victoria Station.

It is not, in fact, so long ago – about two-thirds of a century and within the memory of some people still living – that one could buy a rail ticket with no more formality than handing over the cash, not merely to St Petersburg, but to Bagdad or Basrah, or Peking or Seoul. You could pack a portmanteau, whistle a hansom cab outside your front door, command the driver to take you to Blackfriars or Victoria, or Charing Cross or Liverpool Street, and on arrival install yourself in a few minutes in a *salon privé* on board a *train de luxe*, and alight a fortnight's pleasant journey later in Mukden, Port Arthur, Shanghai or, if you wished to be mundane, Constantinople.

It was a time when a new, wealthy and educated European and American middle class began, thanks to the creation of international expresses, for the first time to explore the world in appreciable numbers, from the fleshpoints of the Riviera to the exotic cities of the extreme Orient.

They did so, by and large, in a luxury unknown before even to royalty, and almost unobtainable since. They travelled on trains equipped with bathrooms, libraries, music rooms, smoking rooms and all manner of comforts completely lost to the international, airborne traveller of today. They stopped over in hotels that were in some cases literally palatial, in that they were converted royal palaces.

It was an extraordinary as well as a grand era of travel, which came to an abrupt end with the outbreak of the First World War, never to be revived.

It is customary for an author to protest that he cannot begin to thank in his preface all those who made his book possible. In this instance, it is unusually true. I can thank Mr Edmund Swinglehurst of Thomas Cook for his kindness, as I can M. Armand Nagelmackers, the libraries of London and Liège Universities, the British Museum and the London staff of Canadian Pacific.

But acknowledgments are due to hundreds of people who

cannot be thanked – those who went by rail into what was then a little-known world and troubled to record their experiences, often anonymously. In deference to them I have aspired, in compiling this book, to allow them to speak for themselves through its pages as much as possible – to act more as introducer and intermediary than as critical interpreter imposing his own view of events on those who actually experienced them. As a widely travelled writer, I have become filled with admiration by the vividness of the mementoes of their journeys that these pioneer travellers left behind. They knew, as modern travellers rarely do, that what they were doing was exciting to others; and they were unquestionably right. Without their painstaking diary-keeping and recording, this book really would not have been possible.

MARTIN PAGE

Compagnie Internationale des Wago

TRAINS EXPR

AVIS AU

La Compagnie Internationale des Wagons-Lits et des Gr
organisé des trains dits " *Express d'Orient.* "

Le nombre des places étant limité, les voyageurs, pou
à l'agence de la Compagnie, à Paris, 3, place de l'Opér

Les voyageurs circulant dans ces trains doivent êt
effectuer. En outre, ces voyageurs, y compris les militai
d'une réduction quelconque sur le chemin de fer, qui em
suppléments indiqués ci-après et qui sont calculés *sur la*

A PLEIN TARIF :

		FR	C.		
	La Ferté-sous-Jouarre . .	2	»	ENTRE	Châl
ENTRE	Épernay	4	35		Bar-l
	Châlons-sur-Marne . . .	5	25	Épernay	Toul
PARIS	Bar-le-Duc	7	70		Nan
	Toul	9	75	et :	Lune
et :	Nancy	10	75		Igne
	Lunéville	11	70	ENTRE	Bar-
	Igney-Avricourt	12	50		Toul
	Epernay	2	35	Châlons-s-Marne	Nan
ENTRE	Châlons-sur-Marne . . .	3	30	et :	Lun
	Bar-le-Duc	5	75		Igne
La Ferté-s.-Jouarre	Toul	7	80	ENTRE	Tou
	Nancy	8	70	Bar-le-Duc	Nan
et :	Lunéville	9	75		Lun
	Igney-Avricourt	10	50	et :	Igne

1. To Constantinople by Steam, 1883

ts et des Grands Express Européens

SS D'ORIENT

PUBLIC

press Européens a l'honneur d'informer le Public qu'elle a

ertains d'y trouver place, devront s'adresser, à l'avance,

s d'un billet de 1ʳᵉ Classe, valable pour le parcours à
arins, les enfants et généralement tous ceux jouissant
ces trains, ont à payer sur les parcours suivants, les
tégrale d'un billet simple de place entière, de 1ʳᵉ classe,

	FR. C.				FR. C.
ne	0 95	**ENTRE**	Nancy		1 05
	3 45	**TOUL**	Lunéville		2 »
	5 45	et :	Igney-Avricourt		2 80
	6 40				
	7 40				
	8 20				
	2 50	**ENTRE**	Lunéville		1 »
	4 50	**NANCY**	Igney-Avricourt		1 80
	5 50	et :			
	6 50				
	7 25	**ENTRE**	Lunéville et Igney-Avricourt.		» 75
	2 »				
	3 05				
	4 05	*Paris, le 15 Novembre 1886.*			
	4 75				

An offer of joy rides on
the Orient Express,
1883.

'Until now, if one has had a fortnight to spare and the mood for an excursion, you might have gone to Fontainebleau or a channel port. Today, you can travel to Constantinople and back, as I've just done.'

Georges Boyer, *Le Figaro*, 1883

On the evening of 4 October 1883 a group of frock-coated gentlemen with revolvers in their pockets assembled on a platform of the Gare de l'Est in Paris.

Attendants in buckled shoes, white stockings and dark-red velvet breeches and monkey-jackets took charge of their bags while they kissed their wives and children – 'We did not part without a little nervousness,' noted one of them in his diary. And they boarded the polished mahogany coaches that gleamed under the new electric chandeliers.

Relatives, friends and onlookers watched through the windows as the travellers installed themselves in their private salons, decorated in the style of Louis XIV, and gazed upon the tables in the restaurant car laid for dinner, with white damask cloths and intricately folded napkins, ornate silverware, hand-blown glasses, the ice buckets already containing champagne and the claret already decanted.

The doors slammed shut. The band stopped playing. The top-hatted stationmaster drew himself to attention. The guard blew his whistle, the crowd gave a cheer and, with a sudden lurch, the train drew out of the station.

As it steamed eastwards away from Paris, the passengers introduced themselves to one another – M. Boyer of *Le Figaro* to M. Opper de Blowitz of *The Times*, M. Olim, a member of the Belgian cabinet, to Missah Effendi, chief secretary of the Turkish Embassy to France, Dr Harzé, the distinguished Parisian physician who was to care for the health of those on board, to General Falciano of Rumania, M. Edmund About, the Alsatian essayist, to M. Grimpel, a rising star of the French Ministry of Finance.

In all they numbered two dozen, including an impeccably mannered Dutchman named Jansson, whose position in life and purpose on board nobody established, Herr von Scala, an Austro-Hungarian official who had breached etiquette by bringing his wife and sister-in-law along, and a watchful clique of bankers who had financed the venture.

The leader of the group was M. Georges Nagelmackers, the young founder of the grandiosely named but still little-known Compagnie Internationale des Wagons-Lits et Grands Express Européens. The occasion was the first journey of the world's first great international train. Nagelmackers's Orient Express, which was to cross central Europe and the brigand-infested Balkans to Constantinople, the capital of the Ottoman Empire, in eighty-two hours.

HORAIRE DU G

Paris-Vienne-Constantinopl

		Arrivée.	Dépa
PARIS....	(London, départ) 10 mat.		7.30
La Ferté-Jouarre	Calais, arrivée. 1.40	8.34 mir.	8.39
Epernay	Calais, départ. 2.16	9.42 »	9.47
Châlons-sur-Marne	Châlons, arriv. 9.35	10.18 »	10.26
Bar-le-Duc		11.41 »	11.45
Toul		12.51 mat.	12.54
Nancy		1.27 »	1.35
Lunéville		2.11 »	2.12
Igney-Avricourt		2.40 »	2.41
Deutsch-Avricourt		2.44 »	
			3.12
Sarrebourg		3.36 »	3.37
Saverne		4.09 »	
Strasbourg		5.02 »	5.07
Kehl		5.29 »	
Appenweier		5.42 »	
Oos (Baden-Baden)		6.22 »	6.26
Carlsruhe		7 »	7.05
Durlach		7.13 »	7.14
Pforzheim		7.48 »	7.50
Mühlacker		8.08 »	Heure
			8.16
Stuttgart		9.18 »	9.23
Geislingen		10.44 »	
Ulm		11.30 »	Heure
			11.45
Augsbourg		1.24 mir.	1 27
München		2.35 »	2.40
Simbach		5 »	Heure
			5.10
Wels		7.04 »	7.10
Amstetten		8.45 »	8.49
Saint-Pölten		9.59 »	10.03
WIEN (West Bahnhof)		11.15 »	11.25
WIEN (Staatsbahnhof)			12.01
Marchegg	1hre de Prague heure de Pest	1.00 mat.	1.04
»		1.18 »	1.22
Pressburg		1.54 »	1.57
Wartberg		2.27 »	2.31
Neuhäusel		3.47 »	3.50
Gross-Nana		4.38 »	4.42
Budapest		6.09 »	6.17
Czegred		7.56 »	8 »
Felegyháza		9.13 »	9.17
Szegedin		10.31 »	10.36
Mokrin		11.29 »	11.33
Hatzfeld		12.14 mid	12.17
Temesvar		1.06 »	1.14
Lugos		2.39 »	2.43
Karansebes		3.36 »	3.40
Porta-Orientalis		4.50 »	4.54
Herkuleshad		5.49 »	5.51
Orsowa		6.16 »	6.23
			Heure
Verciorova		6.30 »	7.43
Turn-Severin		8.07 »	8 09
Craiova		10.50 »	11 »
Slatina		12.24 mid	12.26
Pitesti		2.18 »	2.22
Bukarest		4.45 »	5.18
Giurgevo (Smárda').		6.45 »	
Roustschouk			0.35
Tchernavoda		10.09 mat	10.14
Rasgrad		11.50 »	11.53
Ischiklar		12.31 mid	12.32
Scheytandjik		1.12 »	1.36
Schoumla-Road		2.16 »	2.22
Pravady		3.09 »	3.14
Gubodjin		4.02 »	4.31
VARNA		4.31 »	
» (Lloyd Austro-Hongrois)			6.22
CONSTANTINOPLE	Samedi et Mardi.	6.00 mat.	

NOTA. — *Consulter l'Indicateur des Wagons*

ESS D'ORIENT

onstantinople-Vienne-Paris

		Arrivée.	Départ.	Arrées.
NTINOPLE	Jeudi et Dimanche		12.30 air.	
			5.00 mat.	
		5.29 »	5.30 »	1
		6.22 »	6.27 »	5
Road.		7.15 »	7.20 »	5
k.		8.18 »	8.30 »	12
		9.23 »	9.24 »	1
		9.58 »	9.59 »	1
k.		10.20 »	11.25 »	5
		12.00 soir.		
			1.30 mit.	
Smárda)		3 » »	3.15 »	15
		5.29 »	5.34 »	5
n		7.14 »	7.18 »	4
		8.35 »	8.43 »	3
		11.21 »	11.23 »	2
			Heure de Bucharest.	
		11.43 »	11.25 »	10
ad.		11.34 »	11.44 »	10
talis.		12.09 mat.	12.11 mat	2
		1.12 »	1.16 »	4
		2.13 »	2.17 »	4
		2.58 »	3.02 »	4
		4.15 »	4.23 »	8
			Heure de Pest.	
		5.38 »	5.43 »	5
		6.28 »	6.33 »	5
		7.35 »	7.39 »	4
a		8.37 »	8.41 »	4
		10.02 »	10.08 »	6
		11.25 »	11.28 »	3
		11.50 »	11.54 »	4
		12.14 soir.	12.17 soir.	3
		1.20 »	1.23 »	3
		1.49 »	1.50 »	1
aatsbahnhof)		2.12 »	2.15 »	3
Vestbahnhof)		1.54 »	1.57 »	3
		2.47 »		
		3.20 »	3.25 »	5
		4.40 »	4.44 »	4
		5.54 »	5.58 »	4
		7.33 »	7.39 »	6
			Heure de Munich.	
		9.30 »	9.24 »	5
		11.44 »	11.49 »	5
		12.57 mat	1. » mat	3
			Heure de Stuttgart.	
		2.39 »	2.34 »	5
			Heure de Carlsruhe.	
		4.35 »	4.40 »	5
			Heure de Pau.	
		5.44 »	5.45 »	4
		6.01 »	6.02 »	1
Baden)		6.37 »	6.38 »	1
		6.46 »	6.52 »	6
		7.30 »	7.35 »	8
			Heure de Strasbourg.	
		8.10 »	8.15 »	8
		8.30 »		
		8.48 »	8.53 »	5
		9.44 »		
		10.19 »	10.20 »	1
			Heure française.	
ricourt.		10.43 »	10.21 »	9
court.		10.24 »	10.47 »	23
		11.10 »	11.11 »	1
		11.47 »	11.55 »	8
		12.30 soir.	12.33 mit	3
-Marne.		1.40 »	1.44 »	4
us-Jouarre.		2.53 »	3.01 »	8
		3.35 »	3.40 »	5
		4.48 »	4.52 »	4
		6. » »		

at dans l'horaire du Grand Express d'Orient.

'He is bent on revolutionizing Continental travelling,' Opper de Blowitz, then the doyen not only of the journalists on board but of foreign correspondents everywhere, reported to *The Times*, 'by introducing a comfort and facility hitherto unknown, and has had to struggle for ten years not only against internal difficulties and the conflicting interests of railway companies, but against the indifference of the very portion of the public which is destined to profit from the result.' The ten years of 'internal difficulties' to which Opper referred had included near-bankruptcy and an almost disastrous partnership with an American confidence-trickster. The 'conflicting interests' that had opposed him had embroiled him in tortuous negotiations with ten different railway companies and as many governments.

Mortaged to the hilt though it was before it had even set out, the Orient Express was the result of a thoroughly novel idea, and an unquestioned triumph for Nagelmackers – a supra-national train operated by an individual entrepreneur, running along track and pulled by locomotives belonging to others.

However timorous his guests were at the prospect of being set down, eighty-two hours after their departure from Paris, in a strange and remote eastern city neither they nor many westerners had visited before, and of possibly being attacked on the way by bands of armed robbers (hence their revolvers), they were conscious of partaking in the history of travel. Indeed they were later to publish between them no less than six lengthy accounts of their journey.

Having effected the introductions, everyone set to inspecting the hitherto-unknown comforts of the train that was to take them far beyond the frontiers of western civilization. It was as brand new in its conception as it was in its construction.

There was a smoking room, a ladies' boudoir and a library.

ABOVE The timetable of the Orient Express, 1883. The journey from Paris to Constantinople took four days.

LEFT The Orient Express steaming out of Vienna on its way to Paris.

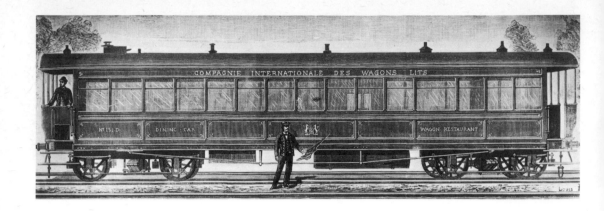

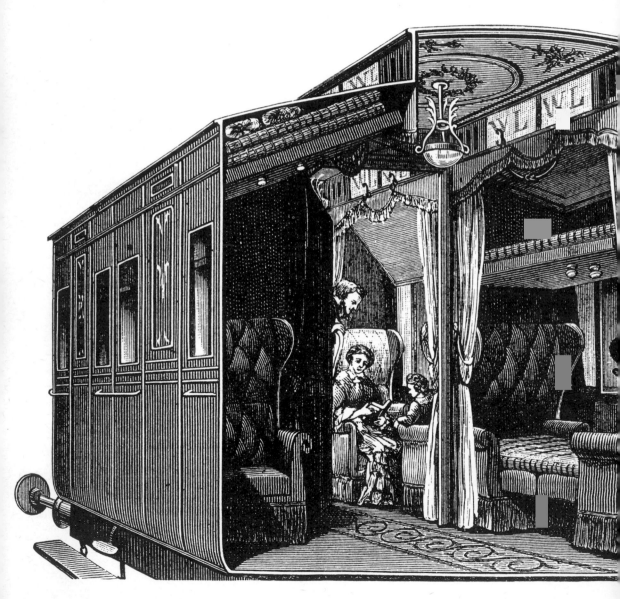

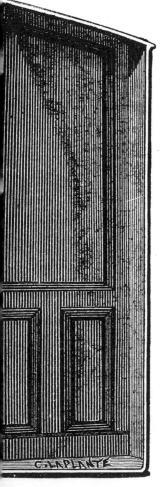

The compartments, or coupés, were miniature drawing rooms with Turkish carpets on the floors, inlaid tables and two red plush armchairs apiece. At night the silk-covered walls folded down to reveal two copiously upholstered beds, transforming each coupé into an equally luxurious sleeping compartment.

Between each coupé was a mosaic-floored *cabinet de toilette*; and in a special coach at the rear of the train, where there were ice-boxes crammed with exotic foods and a servants' dormitory, was a truly remarkable innovation – cubicles containing showers supplied with abundant hot and cold water.

But it was not until the cry of '*Messieurs les voyageurs, le dîner est servi,*' that the travellers saw M. Nagelmackers's *pièce de résistance*. The Orient Express's dining room had a ceiling covered with embossed leather from Cordoue, walls lined with tapestries from the Atelier des Gobelins, founded by the Sun King, and drapes of finest Gênes velvet.

As for the five-course dinner cooked on board from entirely fresh materials by the vast, black-bearded Burgundian chef, Boyer wrote that he was 'not merely of the first order but a man of genius – and my stomach protests such praise to be entirely inadequate'. After the meal the travellers applauded the chef and retired to the smoking room for cigars, whisky and soda and some hands of whist before going to bed.

At speeds of forty miles an hour and more, the Orient Express raced across Europe, through Strasbourg, Vienna and Budapest, greeted at stations along the way by brass bands and local dignitaries. As they drew into Tsigany, in Hungary, a gypsy orchestra came on board, and serenaded them as far as the border. At the end of that dinner the chef emerged from his kitchen, his eyes, according to Opper, 'ablaze with patriotic fervour', and led everyone in a stirring rendering of *La Marseillaise*. Early the next morning they steamed into Bucharest.

Here, their real adventure began. The place had the atmosphere of an exotic frontier town, belatedly stirring itself into the nineteenth century.

'On issuing from the station [wrote Opper] the first thing that strikes you is the cabman, his horse and his vehicle. Here, as throughout the rest of the city, a wonderful contrast forces itself on your notice.

'The cabman, half-barbarian, half-Turk, with a spice of Moujik, cleverly drives small, lean horses which run like the wind over the primitive paving of the suburbs, while the cab, an elegant and comfortable open carriage, would cut a good figure in the Bois de Boulogne.

'Right and left on leaving the station are dingy buildings, mud hovels, worm-eaten shops which display fruit and vegetables, while in the gaps between, the capriciously spaced-out flagstones rest on the bed of slimy mud that forms the interstices.

'As soon, however, as you get through the suburbs, the

ambitious capital strikes the visitor's eye. New and lofty houses, smart and modern, dwarf with their massive upstart splendour the low buildings which adjoin them, and which have not yet emerged from the limbo of the past. A new palace is being erected for the king, but it will be merely temporary, and you perceive the necessity of such a work passing the fissured walls of the old palace, which attempts are being made to repair, and the patching up of which ill-conceals the signs of decay.

'Everywhere is the striking contrast of a city and country which are growing, expanding, embellishing themselves and resolutely marching towards their future destinies. Even on the early hour of Sunday when we arrive, Bucharest is full of

LEFT An Orient Express dinner menu, 6 December 1884, a year after the train was inaugurated.

OPPOSITE Interior of a restaurant car on board the Orient Express.

animation and offers us with its crowded and trimmed-up streets the most motley types of its inhabitants, whose aspect and costume are still lacking in homogeneousness. Yet the top boot here, as in Hungary, is still dominant, showing that the roads have yet to be made and mud is still supreme.

'But if the top boot is still the basis of the national costume, the Astrakhan hat, black, high and pointed, is the summit, while between the basis and the summit, there is free scope for caprice.'

After two hours it was time to return to the station, which most of them did wearing Astrakhans bought in the market.

Back on board the train the travellers were joined by M. Olenescu, Director-General of Rumanian State Railways, who had volunteered to act as their guide and who proved to be an outstanding bore, repeating again and again: 'You do not know it, but our country is worth knowing.'

Just outside Ploesci his tedious harangue was happily interrupted by the sight of a cavalry troop exercising by the side of the railway line.

'It was difficult not to admire [Opper wrote] the precision of their movements, the docility of the horses and the irreproachable bearing of the officers. . . .

'If it chose, or was permitted, the Rumanian Army would speedily cross the Danube on the left, extend its arm on to the right and cross the Varna to Belgrade. I do not say it would be hard to persuade me to the contrary.'

The train climbed slowly upwards through the new oil fields and past red-roofed country inns, into the mountains. Opper and Boyer stood on the footboard, alternately almost freezing

Strasbourg railway station, one of the stopping points of the Orient Express, during the Franco-Prussian War. The war disrupted Nagelmackers's operations almost as soon as they had begun.

in the cold mountain air as they watched the ever-wilder
countryside pass by and then being enveloped by warm smoke
and steam as the train went through a tunnel.

Their destination was Sinaia, the mountain summer resort
recently established by the ruling Hohenzollerns. A small and
remote village before, enormous villas and grand hotels now
sprouted between the carefully ordered flower gardens; and
towering above it all was the new summer palace of King Charles.

As the train drew into the station Opper was delighted to see
his old friend M. Rosetti, president of the Rumanian Chamber
of Commerce in Paris, striding up and down the platform in full
morning dress. Rushing over to greet him, he was more than a
little put out to find that Rosetti was not waiting for him but
had come to fetch M. About to meet His Majesty, a keen
admirer of About's writings, who had learnt that he was passing
through. Opper, whose journalistic style was to grant interviews
to statesmen and monarchs, rather than receive interviews from
them, recovered slightly from this rebuff on hearing that About
would be unable to go to the palace, because he had omitted to
pack court uniform.

With Opper still fretting, the group was taken to Nouls
Hotel, where a lavish buffet had been laid for them on a terrace
overlooking the resort. Another gypsy orchestra serenaded them,
which Opper sourly compared with the worst musicians of
Naples.

Those of the party in better spirits were about to start dancing
on the lawn, when one of the King's *aides-de-camp* approached
with a message inviting them all (dressed as they were) to the
summer palace, where the formal opening ceremony was taking
place at that moment.

Opper became cheerful again, and later wrote:

'We were not very presentable on leaving the hotel, hot and
travel weary, but we were less so on reaching the gates of the
summer Palace. It was raining, and from the hotel to the Palace
we had to traverse a mile and a half of a road cut up by the carts
which, during years of building operations had brought, as it
were bit by bit, the mansion now inaugurated. . . .

'A troup of people had collected at the gates, soldiers and
officers were marching up and down, and Greek priests, holding
up their black robes to avoid the mud, their dark beards dripping
with rain and their hoods dangling down limp and sodden, were
leaving the royal dwelling where the ceremony was just over.

'When we arrived, our clothes soaked and our boots covered
in mud, the flunkies in livery on the ground floor and the soldiers
mounting guard beheld us with stupefaction and suspicion.

'An orderly officer, informed of the royal command, procured
us admission, we entered the ante-room, deposited our umbrellas
and cloaks; and our forty pairs of boots, weighted by the mud
from the road, resounded like thunder on the stairs.'

All too aware of their decrepitude amid the grandeur, the travellers held themselves back in the audience room, with the exception of the impossible Opper, who promptly had himself introduced to the Queen. By his own account, the latter was entranced by his company – 'We talk of all that the Queen loves: poetry, literature, art, for not only is she a felicitous writer, but she has a talent for painting and is very clever at illuminating.' Opper was feeling in his element, and when Her Majesty remarked that she had adopted Rumanian national dress as the court costume for ladies, to benefit local workshops instead of Parisian couturiers, he went so far as to venture a simpering pleasantry:

'I cannot help saying, with a smile: "Your Majesty's patriotism would seem much more meritorious if the costume did not become you so well."

"You are sceptical," replied the Queen, smiling in her turn, "and you do not think me capable of sacrificing elegance for patriotism."

"Heaven forbid, Madame," I rejoined. "The costume becomes both the women and the Queen. It is fortunate when there is no incompatibility between the rights of the one and the duties of the other."'

At this point the King, apparently having inquired who this short, fat, small-headed, unkempt stranger talking familiarly with his wife might be, sent a courtier to fetch him over.

Charles asked whether it was not true that he had been awarded the Star of Rumania for his reportage of the Congress of Berlin: 'I bowed, and after a few seconds raised my head.' 'Your Majesty no doubt felt no reason to complain of the results of the Congress?' he ventured, and embarked on a lengthy account, the details of which the King was already more than acquainted with, of Rumania's outcome from the negotiations. His Majesty replied somewhat brusquely that it would take ten years of hard work to begin to produce any benefits from the territories gained. Opper cheerfully riposted: 'Prince Bismarck, Your Majesty, replying to a diplomatist who asked how long he thought peace would last, said about ten years.' 'He made that remark five years ago,' the King replied, and shortly proposed to Opper that he should now join the others on a guided tour of the new palace.

During their promenade through the public rooms, which included a public billiards hall – probably a unique feature for a palace – the King was apparently prevailed upon to realize that it was ill-advised to make an enemy of Opper de Blowitz of *The Times*. Another courtier was dispatched to invite him to take tea with His Majesty, during which the latter listened with exemplary patience to the journalist's views on the situation in the Balkans, a part of the world he had arrived in that day and never visited before.

On board the train once more, the travellers dined on Rumanian caviar, compared with which, Opper opined, the Russian variety was but boot leather. They journeyed through the night to the crossing point on the River Danube.

It was to be another six years before all the necessary bridges were built and the track was laid to permit trains to run straight through from Paris to Constantinople, and here the party had to leave the western Orient Express of M. Nagelmackers, and board the eastern one operated by the Austrian Oriental Railways. As the train steamed towards the landing stage they looked across the river to Giurgevo on the Bulgarian side and were overcome with a not entirely pleasant feeling that civilization had petered away some miles back.

'A troup of Roumanians, ragged and repulsive looking, rushed at the carriages to carry our bags to the steamer; but a lusty cry resounded along the train: "Do not give up your luggage except to the porters in livery, otherwise you will never see it again."'

On board the ferry, they gazed at the new train awaiting them and the railway employees 'lolling lazily along its length, watching stoically as the boat approaches'. Halfway across M. Lechat, M. Nagelmackers's secretary, handed over responsibility for the party to Herr Wiener, his Austrian opposite number. He did so with the mocking cry of: 'Look at these splendid Bulgars of yours! See how enthusiastically they prepare for our arrival!'

At Sinaia the day before one of the ladies-in-waiting had presented posies to the two women in the party, Frau von Scala and her sister. Now, as they walked down the gangplank on to Bulgarian soil, a customs officer came up and confiscated them. 'We stared at him,' Opper reported, 'amazed at such a proceeding, but the official with a confused and humble air said: "Phylloxera! Phylloxera!" and was stupified by the roar of laughter following his explanation.'

On the station platform a fine sight met their eyes – 'a handsome officer in splendid costume, walking up and down'. Opper claimed that 'this imposing specimen stalks up and down, however, by order, at the arrival and departure of every train – viz four times a week. That is his function – to be a deceptive specimen of an imaginary army.'

Opper and Boyer caught a glimpse of the real Bulgarian army by hiring a carriage to take them into the nearby city of Rustchuk – 'that strange town of hovels and cellars which shelters 25,000 people and resembles a settlement of troglodytes. Soldiers – ill-equipped, sluggish and disordered – were manoeuvring on the square as we drove round.'

Boyer took up the tale:

'The Russian officer who was supposed to be instructing them ordered them to stand at ease. Forthwith, we heard a strange sound.

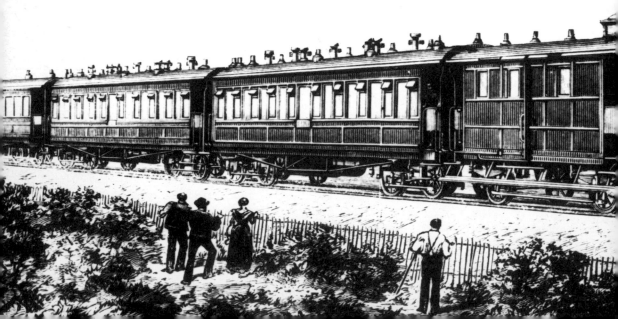

Nagelmackers's improved design for an international railway coach, which he exhibited at the Paris Exhibition of 1878 and introduced in the Orient Express soon afterwards.

'With admirable precision and co-ordination, all the troopers simultaneously blew their noses into their hands.'

Time was up, and they raced back to the station. Arriving in the forecourt, the driver 'stiffened his legs against the footboard, leaned back and pulled at the reins with all his might, and stopped the horses with a force strong enough to dislocate their jaws or break their legs'.

The eastern Orient Express soon passed into brigand country. At Votova Station, where they stopped, they learnt that a particularly bloodthirsty gang had attacked less than a fortnight before.

'They smeared the woodwork with petroleum [Opper reported] and garotted the stationmaster and his subordinates in order to get hold of the money they expected to find in his till. They severely maltreated and were near to scalping him, carried off his daughter, a girl of thirteen, and would have burnt him alive with the station had they not by the purest chance been alarmed by some workmen coming back in trucks. . . .'

The travellers took their revolvers from their holsters, slid off the safety catches and, clutching their weapons, resumed their places.

No attack came, but that was about all they could favourably say of Bulgaria and the Bulgarians. Opper wrote of a journey through countryside of

'. . . the most barren and melancholy monotony. Untilled fields, stunted bushes, sandy or sloppy soil. Now and then there is a Bulgarian cemetery, where some miserable goat, some mangy buffalo, is browsing as though human bodies alone were capable of manuring this refractory soil. At times, straggling along a petty stream, there is a village consisting of miserable cottages, bordered by mud hovels, riddled with holes, which serve as coverts for gypsies.'

They stopped to lunch at the station buffet at Scheytandjik, where the food and wine were unanimously agreed to be atrocious. Opper persuaded Boyer to order roasted guinea-fowl, and apologetically recorded how his colleague 'nearly died of starvation, trying to eat the bird, which was made of artificial marble. He was still struggling with all his might to tame it, when the signal was given for our departure.'

As the train moved on its way Opper recorded his 'stupefaction' that Lord Beaconsfield once nearly went to war over Bulgaria, and that the royal family did not 'leap at the slightest opportunity of leaving this ungrateful soil'. Arriving in the port of Varna, where they were to board an Austrian Lloyd steam-packet for the last portion of the journey, they were surrounded by hordes of beggars – men, women and disfigured infants. The harbour itself was thoroughly dilapidated and so ill dredged that the ship's master refused to bring the vessel alongside the quay. Varna had been ceded to Bulgaria at the Congress of Berlin, and all the nation had done with its prize, Opper thundered, 'is to institute the most vexatious customs regulations to the irritation of the traveller who embarks or lands there at the risk of drowning'.

Peasants admiring the Orient Express passing in 1883.

The weather was rough, and the 'clumsy boats and noisy boatmen' who took them to the steamer made them fear for their lives. To board the ship, as well as to leave the dockside, it was necessary to use rope ladders, greatly increasing the passengers' terror. To add insult to danger, they were charged a hefty port levy for the use of the facilities.

The voyage down the Black Sea coast lasted eighteen hours, most of which Opper spent in his cabin being sick. But as the ship neared the Golden Horn he was persuaded to join the rest of the party on the foredeck, to catch a first glimpse of the Bosporus and Constantinople itself. 'Our first sight of it was not particularly seductive,' Boyer recorded. 'Lots of little houses discordantly painted yellow or dirty pink with their shutters closed, gave not a grandiose but a strange impression.'

Opper simply burst into a roar of supercilious laughter which, he later explained, was occasioned by the discrepancy between the glamorous pictures he had seen and accounts he had read of the view, and the actuality of the squalor before his eyes.

The ship turned a little in the water and Opper was suddenly silenced. According to Boyer, 'it was as though a vast theatre curtain had risen and we were facing the real Constantinople. The ancient Turkish city was wrapped in a gauze of transparent mist, through which we saw the mosques, with their minarets like great church candles. . . . All our dreams were surpassed by the splendour and beauty.'

It was in elated mood that the Orient Express's first passengers disembarked at Top-Hani, the artillery headquarters made available to them as a landing place by the Sultan in commemoration of their historic journey.

They drove in landaus to Pera, the diplomatic quarter, and drew up outside the Grand Hotel – a place grand only in name.

Without delay, Opper applied himself to the task of lobbying, wheedling, pushing and ingratiating his way into an audience with the Sultan, who had never granted an interview to the press in his life. The others, taking a more relaxed view of their visit, delivered themselves into the care of Saker Ahmed Pasha, whom His Majesty had deputed to look after them throughout their stay.

He took them on a tour of the royal palaces – magnificent marbled edifices but, in Boyer's view, somewhat vulgar and florid. They were shown the mansion built for the Empress Eugénie during her stay in the Ottoman capital and admired the white marble bathroom, 'as big as the foyer of the Opéra-Comique in Paris but unfortunately, at the time of our visit, empty'. In the gardens, they saw the miniature zoo with caged tigers.

The festival of Iduladha, which commemorates Abraham's sacrifice to God, was about to begin. Local colour was added to the hotel lobby by the presence there of sheep wandering about,

24

TEN MINUTES F

REFRESHMENTS.

unknowingly awaiting their turn to be sacrificially slaughtered. And it was the time of year when the Sultan publicly humbled himself before God.

In reality the act of devotion was public more in letter than in spirit. Each year the Sultan underwent his ceremony of humiliation in a different mosque, and the one he had chosen was kept as a guarded palace secret until the very last moment, when it was too late for a large crowd to gather.

His Majesty did, however, obligingly send word to the hotel, advising the foreigners where to go. Opper declined the invitation for fear that his presence in a group of sightseers might cause him to lose face with the court; the rest of them went along.

The Sultan arrived at the entrance of the mosque to thin cheers from a tiny crowd of Turks. Inside they could hear a choir chanting: 'Beware lest the homage paid to you makes you proud. There is but one God who is greater by far than you.' After the service, from which the visitors were excluded as non-Moslems, the Sultan re-emerged from the mosque in procession, on horseback. Immediately before him rode the Grand Vizier and, behind, the chief of the black eunuchs.

Then they went to see the whirling dervishes go through their extraordinary rite, made a tour of archaeological sites and began the journey home again – Opper complete with his report of the Sultan's first-ever interview with a journalist, which predictably devoted more space to its author's remarks to the Sultan than to the Sultan's remarks to the author.

Arriving back in Rustchuk, they were amused to see the same officer, bedecked in finery, pacing up and down the platform, and elated to see Nagelmackers's train, symbolizing civilization and all its comforts, awaiting them on the other bank.

Their numbers swelled by a United States senator, who caused considerable irritation by disparaging the speed of the Orient Express compared with that of American trains, they journeyed uneventfully to Vienna, where they were joined by the Orient Express's first fare-paying passengers. Most, according to Opper, were beautiful and elegant young women; and the restaurant car for the rest of the journey became 'animated with the sound of their silvery voices'. The corridors 'became like the pavement of the Rue de la Paix. The beautiful young ladies emerged from their compartments impeccably turned out, to promenade under the scrutiny of the male passengers.'

The Orient Express arrived at the French border several hours late. The French driver, having had ample leisure to build up steam pressure to its maximum, now used this to speed the train across the countryside at such a pace that even the senator was silenced, and they drew into the Gare de l'Est exactly on time, to find a commemorative banquet awaiting them.

The world's first grand railway adventure was over, and the era of the great international train had begun.

OPPOSITE Queen Victoria's carriage. Her willingness to travel by train did much to make railway travel a respectable amusement for the moneyed classes.

George Pullman lured passengers on board his palace cars with glamorized advertisements like this.

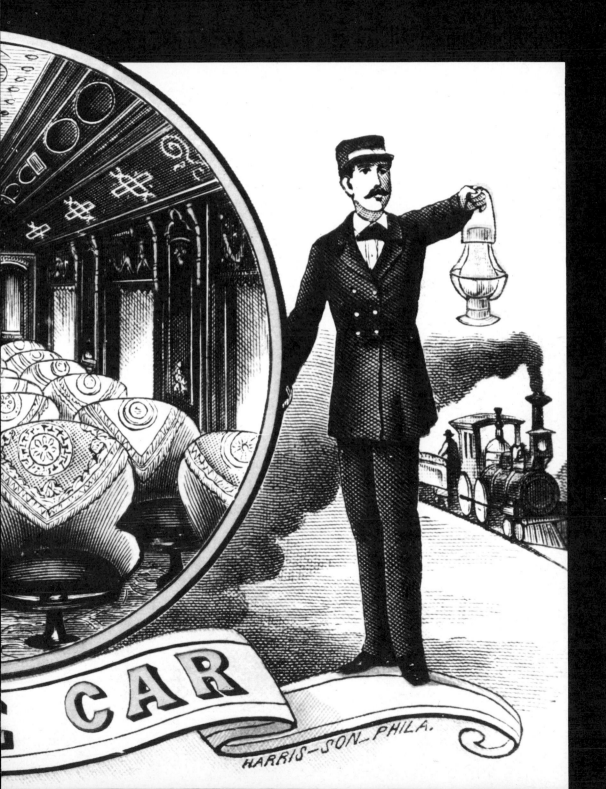

CAR

HARRIS-SON-PHILA.

One man dominated the great era of international travel in *trains de luxe* that opened with the inauguration of the Orient Express and flourished until the outbreak of the First World War in 1914, thirty years later. He was a handsome, long-faced Belgian with the cumbersome name of Georges Nagelmackers, who founded La Compagnie Internationale des Wagons-Lits et Grands Express Européens when he was but twenty-four years old.

His remarkable career as creator and operator of the world's finest and most famous trains had a bizarre beginning. He was born in Liège, in 1845, into a family that proudly traced its lineage back to the Middle Ages and enjoyed good relations with the monarchy. His father, a banker, helped finance the morally dubious business ventures of the scoundrelly Leopold II, King of All the Belgians and, as it was unkindly but aptly added, Most of the Money. His mother was a member of one of the country's most élite families, the Frère-Orbans.

Georges became an independent entrepreneur because he

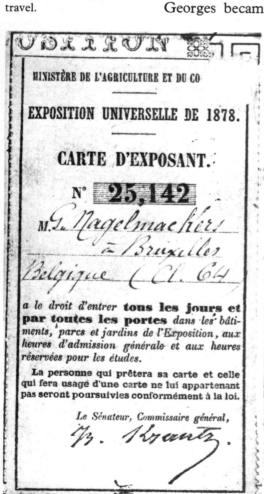

George Nagelmackers, the remarkable Belgian entrepreneur who founded La Compagnie Internationale and dominated the great era of international rail travel.

George Mortimer
Pullman. His historic
success was founded on
selling phoney luxury.
In reality his carriages
were usually crowded
and uncomfortable.

fell in love at the age of twenty-one with an older woman, who
spurned him in some amusement. He took the rejection extremely hard, and hurriedly sailed from the scene of his humiliation to New York.

The United States was not only the most distant place that
could be reached conveniently from Europe. It also had already
gained the reputation of being a mechanical wonderland, where
inventing was the national passion, and the most overworked
civil servants in Washington were those engaged by the Patents
Office. Abroad, ebullient American claims to be a generation in
advance of anywhere else in matters technical were uncritically
accepted at face value. European visitors, especially journalists,
were flocking to the New World to inspect its latest man-made
wonders – and, in particular, to ride on its revolutionary new
passenger trains.

In the Europe of those days hardly anyone ventured more
than a few hours from home. In the United States the transcontinental railroad was nearing completion at a staggering pace

33

of one and a half miles of new track laid a day in each direction. The settled regions were already crisscrossed with lines, and journeys of a week or more were becoming almost commonplace.

In reporters' accounts American trains were imbued with a splendour that rivalled the most magnificent ocean liners. Coaches were decked out in finery – ornately inlaid panelling, embroidered upholstery, cut-glass mirrors. There were conveyances called sleeping cars, unknown in the rest of the world, which contained beds for night travel. Only a few months before Nagelmackers's arrival George Mortimer Pullman had unveiled to an astonished public his latest triumph: the 'Delmonico' dining car, the first-ever restaurant on wheels, on board which one could sit at a table eating fresh-fried oysters and broiled beefsteak, as the countryside passed by the windows.

To distract himself, Nagelmackers soon joined the ranks of the railway sightseers, and he became so much diverted that he extended his emotional convalescence for eighteen months while the idea to perfect passenger travel formed in his mind.

In fact, as Nagelmackers soon found out, the press on both sides of the Atlantic, in proclaiming that the age of great American trains had arrived, was anticipating events by about half a century. Journalists in those days were more scrupulous than they are now in repaying favours received in column inches of glowing prose; and the largesse of Mr Pullman's hospitality, particularly, knew few bounds. From the contemporary accounts of more disinterested travellers, journeying through the United States was usually an uncomfortable and often a wretched experience.

It was to be some years before dining cars came into widespread use, and Mr Pullman's Delmonico car was far from being the final answer to a hungry traveller's prayers – as he unabashedly stated in his patent application, the kitchen was placed in the middle, so that in no matter which direction the train travelled only half the customers would have to put up with the smoke and fumes from the cooking.

Meals were generally taken at station buffets. According to the timetables, passengers were given twenty minutes in which to eat. In reality the train's conductor, 'that exceedingly self-satisfied monarch', as Mark Twain called him, who devoted his talents 'to the invention of new methods of discommoding and snubbing you', not infrequently took bribes from the buffet's owner to blow the whistle for departure in advance. This was to ensure that travellers, having paid for their food, should have the minimum of opportunity to consume it, so that it could be saved and resold to the next trainload of suckers.

Those who did contrive to eat their meals were less than pleased with the quality. Twain wrote of 'five-minute boltings of flabby rolls, muddy coffee, questionable eggs, gutta-percha beef, and pies whose conception and execution are a dark and bloody mystery'. An English traveller, J.W.Boddam-Wetham recounted:

'As a rule the food is ill-cooked and worse served. Morning, noon and night the same cry greets you: mutton chop, beefsteak, ham and eggs. No change of any sort from the time you leave New York until you arrive in San Francisco.

'There are desperate skirmishes with the waiter, who persists in bringing tea when you want coffee and who tells you: "It's all the same, sir"; the struggles for the bread or sugar and the hateful cry of "All aboard" ringing in your ear and obliging you to rush off, leaving the proprietor counting his money and arranging the victuals for the next batch.

'It is wonderful how expert the people who keep these places become in collecting money.'

Lest these remarks be dismissed as those of two especially cantankerous individuals, let me quote from an editorial of the period, in the *New York Times*:

'If there is any word in the English language more shamefully misused than another, it is the word refreshment, as applied to the hurry-scurry of eating and drinking at railroad stations. The dreary places in which the painful and unhealthy performances take place are called Refreshment Saloons, but there could not be a more inappropriate designation for such abominations of desolation.

'Directors of railroad companies appear to have an idea that travellers are destitute of stomach; that eating and drinking are not at all necessary to human beings bound on long journeys; and that nothing more is required than to put them through their misery in as brief a time as possible.

'It is expected that three or four hundred men, women and children, some of whom must, of necessity, be feeble folk and unaccustomed to roughing it, and all of whom have been used to decencies and comforts of orderly homes, can be whirled half a day over a dusty road, with hot cinders flying in their faces; and then when they approach a station dying of weariness, hunger and thirst, longing for an opportunity to bathe their faces at least before partaking of their much-needed refreshments, that they shall rush out helter-skelter into a dismal, long room and dispatch a supper, breakfast or dinner in fifteen minutes.

'The consequences of such savage and unnatural feeding are not reported by telegraph as railroad disasters, but if a faithful account were taken of them we are afraid that they would be found much more serious than any that are caused by the smashing of cars or the breaking of bridges. The traveller who has been riding all night in a dusty and crowded car, unable to sleep, and half suffocated with smoke and foul air, will be suddenly roused from his half-lethargic condition by hearing the scream of the steam whistle, which tells of the near approach

OVERLEAF A ticket inspector – 'that exceedingly self-satisfied monarch', as Mark Twain called him – disrupting the repose of passengers at night in order to cram another two people into the already overcrowded coach. From *America Revisited* (1883) by George Augustus Sala.

to a station; but before the train stops, the door of the car opens and the conductor shouts at the top of his voice: 'Pogramville – fifteen minutes for breakfast!'

'Here is a prospect for a weary and hungry traveller to whom fifteen minutes would be brief time enough for ablutions. But washing is out of the question, even if all the conveniences were at hand, and he rushes into the "saloon" where he is offered a choice of fried ham and eggs, or rough beefsteak soaked in bad butter, tea and coffee, stale bread; the inevitable custard pie and pound cake are also at his service; but half the fifteen minutes allowed for breakfast having been lost while waiting for a turn at one of the two washbasins, the bewildered traveller makes a hasty grab at whatever comes within his reach, and hurries back to his seat, to discover before he reaches the end of his journey, that he has laid the foundations for a fit of dyspepsia, which may lead to a disease of the lungs or a fever.

'. . . As affairs are now arranged, a few days of railroad travelling are sure to end in a fit of sickness of all excepting those who have hearty constitutions, and are accustomed to the very roughest and toughest manner of living.'

ABOVE Pullman's sleeping railway car. The ornate exterior concealed the interior squalor.

LEFT and RIGHT Two illustrations from *America Revisited*: LEFT preparing for bed in a Pullman sleeping car. The passengers handed over their boots to the conductor, not primarily to have them cleaned, but to reduce the chances of their being stolen.

RIGHT Morning toilet: a single faucet served an entire coachload.

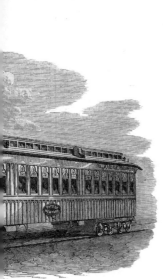

On board the trains themselves, conditions were no better. Even in first-class day coaches the seats were narrow and hard, with low backs, and one was jolted severely by the motion of the train. In the 'sleeping cars' – in quality mobile dormitories – the bunks were so cramped and uncomfortable as to render sleep as impossible as it was undesirable, given that one's boots, fob watch and Smith and Wesson were quite likely to be stolen if one did doze off.

One English traveller, C.B. Berry, complained: 'We had heard a good deal about the marvellous luxury and convenience of American trains and had been given to understand that a journey in the States was an experience of almost ecstatic bliss: "For unparalleled upholstery, the profusion of comfort and civility of employees, our cars are without a compeer; no other cars are a patch upon them. . . ." ' Boarding one of these magnificent conveyances for the first time, Berry recounted how he found

'. . . the atmosphere resembled that of a lime kiln, dry and baking, the effect of a large stove at each end, aggravated by the windows' being closely shut. The car had no division from end

to end, a length of some fifty feet, while to light this huge apartment the Pennsylvania Railroad had generously provided two candles swung in glass globes as in the stateroom of a steamer. The dim religious light provided sufficient just to exhibit the extent of the darkness and was well suited to such as might desire sleep, but 6 PM was rather early for a car full of people to seek repose. Then, as if in playful irony, a newsman appeared offering newspapers and magazines for sale.

'Sleep would have been perilous, since from the lowness of the seat backs the sleeper's head would have descended to the rear in an uncertain and suicidal manner.'

As for the wonders wrought by George Mortimer Pullman, J. W. Boddam-Whetham reported:

'The man who slept in the berth next to mine snored frightfully; in fact, the night was made hideous by the unmusical sounds issuing from all parts of the car. The horrors of that first night in a Pullman car are indelibly impressed on my mind. The atmosphere ran a close heat with that of the Black Hole of Calcutta. On my asking the porter why he kept a fire burning all night he said he had to sit up and it would never do for him to catch cold.

'If going to bed is a misery, getting up in the morning is simply agony. If you are late, you have to wait some hours before you can get a turn at the washbasin. If you are early, you have to stand outside on the platform in the dust and smoke until the beds are once more metamorphosed into seats, there being no other place to retire to until the operation is performed.'

Another early and dissatisfied Pullman customer was Horace Greely:

'There were two high berths to choose from; both wicker trays, ledged in, cushioned and rugged. The one was about a foot and a half higher than the other, so I chose the top one as being nearer the zinc ventilator . . .

'I clambered to my perch and found it was like lying on one's back on a narrow plank. If I turned my back to the car wall the motion of the train bumped me off my bed altogether and if I turned my face to the wall I felt a horrible sensation of being likely to roll backward into the aisle, so I lay on my back and settled the question. It was like trying to sleep on the back of a runaway horse. . . .'

'You have to go to bed in your boots,' recounted the Viscountess Avon. 'Indeed, you cannot undress at all because you cannot shroud yourself behind the curtains without placing yourself in a recumbent position. Besides, what could be done with one's clothing?'

James Hogan, an Australian writer, related a story of a lady who did disrobe on board a sleeping car:

'Resolving to obtain coolness at any cost, she violently kicked off her blankets, but in doing so, she unfortunately overlooked the fact that her own clothes were stacked near the window that she had thrown open before retiring in order to admit some fresh air. Thus it was that in her struggles to cool herself she inadvertently kicked her wearing apparel out of the window, with the embarrassing result that next morning she was constrained to make her appearance attired in a hat, stockings and a blanket.'

The bunks were packed so tightly together that it was far from unknown to wake up to find one's neighbour's feet resting on one's face. The atmosphere was such as to induce frequent headaches. The provision of sheets and pillows was a comparatively recent innovation unavailable in most sleepers; and the cleanliness of the blankets was suspect.

It was all a very far cry indeed from the publicists' and journalists' gushing account of the opulent life to be enjoyed on board the 'palaces on wheels'. As Lady Avon, a redoubtable and hardy traveller despite her aristocratic status, who roamed over much of the world taking little more than her carpet bag and her always ready-to-hand whisky flask, remarked: 'I think that few people who have spent a week in one of these palaces would ever wish to spend another.' And as for the superiority of American trains over those of the Old World, we have the testimony of Mark Twain, who was nobody's man, that in Europe the carriages were more comfortable, the ride smoother, the railway officials many times more courteous and solicitous, the meal-breaks adequate and the cooking at station refreshment rooms superb. It is true that he cavilled at the absence of sleeping cars; but the lack of a plank-type bunk on which to be stifled and jolted through the night seems a small loss when weighed against the other comforts afforded.

By coincidence, Mark Twain was in Europe as a member of his famous group of 'innocents abroad' in the same year – 1867 – that Georges Nagelmackers came the other way across the Atlantic to the United States. It did not take Nagelmackers long to discover how skin deep was the beauty of American trains and how lamentably they failed to serve the wants of the affluent new middle classes, spawned by the industrial revolution and filled with the desire to travel if only they were provided with the means to do so. Within a few years he was to stand up against Pullman in his own home territory of Europe and rout him completely, as the upstart, by the worthy expedient of actually providing what Pullman pretended to offer. More immediately, the question that must be answered is how Pullman, despite the evidence, became a name ranked with Rolls and Royce and Ritz as being synonymous with the last word in luxury and refinement.

E. Hamilton Ellis, the distinguished British railway historian, once said of George Mortimer Pullman that he was 'one per cent inventor, nine per cent businessman and ninety per cent publicist'. Even this jaundiced assessment may have been over-generous – aware of his own curtness and ill-concealed disdain for journalists, and indeed for the travelling public, he entrusted the promotional side of the business to his more affable brother Albert, one of the first and most masterful of modern public relations men.

Pullman used to assert – or rather, Albert used to assert on his behalf – that he became determined to go into the sleeping-car business and indeed to revolutionize it as a result of a memorably dreadful rail journey from Chicago to New York.

The interior of a Pullman drawing-room car. The seats were ornately upholstered but hard to sit upon.

The truth was otherwise. Pullman's father was a carpenter who taught himself the trade of moving whole buildings from one site to another, to facilitate road widening and other public works. As a young man George did not display a talent for following in his father's footsteps, or for acquiring any other skill, and his parents obtained him a position as a store clerk. Then his father fell ill in the middle of an important contract, called George into the business and left it to him when he died soon afterwards.

Despite a lucrative assignment in Chicago, involving the raising of a hotel complete with furniture and guests – a procedure that Pullman supervised at a safe, shouting distance from his foreman and workers – the business did not prosper for long, and he soon had cause for concern about his future.

While working on a small project in Albion, New York State, Pullman had the good fortune to meet and be befriended by Benjamin Field, a one-time New York State senator, and his brother Norman. Soon afterwards the Field brothers were awarded a contract to operate sleeping cars on the Chicago and Alton and the Galena and Chicago Union railroads; and they invited Pullman to join them in the venture in the capacity of fitter.

Two obsolescent day cars were bought, and Pullman and a mate worked on them through much of 1858, converting them into what amounted to twenty-bunk dormitories. Already displaying his preference for flamboyance at the expense of creature comfort, he expensively clad the cars in cherrywood, much as the owner of a sideshow in a fairground spends more on the outside display than on the attractions within. In fitting the interior Pullman worked to no blueprint, improvising the design as he progressed and working out the measurements as he came to them. The result was much as might have been expected from such a procedure: a pair of the most ill-conceived and unsatisfactory sleeping cars in America.

'It was a primitive thing [said Mr J.L.Barnes, conductor of one of the first two cars to be built by the man who has so often and so falsely been attributed with the invention of sleeping cars]. Besides being lighted with candles it was heated by a stove at the end of each car. There were no carpets on the floor and the interior of the car was arranged in this way: the backs of the seats were hinged and to make up the lower berth, the porter merely dropped the back of the seat until it was level with the back itself. Upon this, he placed a mattress and a blanket. There were no sheets . . .

'The car had a very low deck and was quite short. It had four-wheel trucks and with the exception of the springs under it was similar to the freight car of today . . . the washbasin was made of tin. The water for the washbasin came from the drinking can which had a faucet so that people could get a drink.'

There were so few takers at fifty cents per night over and above the normal fare that the income was not sufficient even to cover Mr Barnes's wages for collecting the surcharge, and he was soon fired in a very necessary economy drive.

The Field and Pullman Sleeping Car Company was offered an honourable escape from bankruptcy by the outbreak of civil war, at which the Union Army, no doubt to the partners' relief, requisitioned its sleeping cars for use as troop transports. Pullman himself did not answer the call to arms, and moved instead as far from the war as possible. He ended up in Gregory Gulch, Colorado, where he reverted to his original career of store keeper, selling provisions brought in from Denver, at mark-ups of up to 1,000 per cent, to gold prospectors.

By the time the war was over he had amassed a sizeable fortune and returned to Chicago to re-establish himself as an entrepreneur of sleeping cars, having somehow ditched the Field brothers in the meantime. Armed with his acquired wealth, he bought a workshop and set about building from scratch what he vowed would be the finest conveyance America and the world had ever known.

Its name, the 'Pioneer', he borrowed from the Chicago and Alton's most famous locomotive. The decor of inlaid walnut panels, ornate mirrors and polished brass rails he borrowed from the Mississippi steamboats. The embroidered upholstery would have looked well in a Fifth Avenue drawing room. In all

LEFT An early photograph of Pullman cars under construction.

BELOW The Pioneer, intended by Pullman to be the grandest and biggest car on the rails. He built it with the assistance of two carpenters, improvising the design as work progressed. The railway companies regarded it as an anachronism but it found success when it transported Abraham Lincoln's body from Washington to his native Springfield.

45

he spent the massive sum of $20,000, ten times more than his first cars had cost; and once again most of it went on an exterior in the apparent belief that it would somehow compensate for the lack of decent accommodation.

This time Pullman had worked to a pre-arranged design. But in his enthusiasm to produce not only the grandest but also the biggest car on the rails, he had overlooked the point that there was no railroad in the United States that could convey such a huge vehicle. The Chicago and Alton and Galena and Chicago Union railroads pointed out this objection to him, and declined to introduce the Pioneer into service.

To put it bluntly, Pullman was saved from the consequences of his folly by the assassination of President Abraham Lincoln. Lincoln's body was to be transported from Washington to his hometown of Springfield. Colonel James H. Bowen of Chicago was charged with making the arrangements for the rail cortège for the final sector of the journey. He was also, as president of Chicago's Third National, Pullman's banker; and Pullman, as a result of his ill-gotten gains from the Colorado goldrush, was one of his major depositors. Colonel Bowen adamantly insisted, against the protests of the railroad involved, the Chicago and Alton, that the only suitable conveyance was the Pioneer car. If the car did not fit the railroad, then the railroad must be adapted to suit the car. The railroad's directors, faced with the alternative of being charged with lack of patriotism and a proper sense of grief, hurriedly, if seethingly, had the bridges strengthened, the cuttings broadened and the station platforms drawn back from the line to accommodate Pullman's car.

With the President's coffin on board, the train set off on its slow journey, the locomotive engineer dolefully tolling his bell as he went. Along the route the entire populations of towns and villages turned out to pay their last respects and, incidentally, to gaze upon the Pioneer car; and Pullman's publicity gain was stupendous.

His exploitation of Lincoln's funeral did not stop there. On its return journey he had the Pioneer shunted into sidings all along the way, and put on public exhibition. Free rides in it were given to local journalists and dignitaries; the published and public comments about the car that had been used as the President's railroad hearse were suitably reverent; and it was not long before the Chicago and Alton's directors felt obliged to put it into regular service.

Soon afterwards he found the opportunity to inveigle his other old customer, the Galena and Chicago Union, now re-named the Michigan Central, in a not dissimilar fashion. Galena was the hometown of Ulysses Grant, and it was not long after Lincoln's funeral that he began his progress there to receive a returning hero's welcome.

On receiving the news that Grant had reached Detroit,

A poster advertising the Chicago and Alton Railroad, who were forced by a skilful public relations campaign organized by George Pullman to use his Pioneer car. They had to make considerable alterations to the railroad to accommodate it.

Pullman rushed the Pioneer there, offered the free use of it to Grant for the remainder of his journey and gained a ready acceptance. Again Pullman seized the chance to show off the car, when Grant was not using it and during its return trip. Another blaze of fulsome publicity was thus engineered, forcing the hand of the Michigan Central's directors into signing a contract.

Under such relentless promotional pressures one railroad after another succumbed. From the Pioneer he graduated to the 'Palace' car – still more opulent in its display, if hardly more comfortable in its appointments; and his greatest breakthrough came with the battle to gain the sleeping-car business of the Union Pacific, soon to be part of the transcontinental line.

Palace Car life on the Pacific Railroad, 1879. Pullman deftly outmanoeuvred Andrew Carnegie in capturing the lucrative West Coast market.

47

An early restaurant car. Pullman was a pioneer in providing passengers with hot meals on board trains.

His opponent for the contract was no less a figure than Andrew Carnegie, in this case representing the Central Transportation Company, which owned the rights in the sleeping cars designed by the older-established and more reputable Wagner organization. Early in the negotiations it was clear to Carnegie that Pullman, helped not a little by the Barnum and Bailey publicity tactics employed by Albert, was winning the day; and all the former could do was to plead for an adjournment of the decision. In the meantime he saw sense. Pullman, he wrote later, 'was one of those characters who could see the drift of things, and was always swimming in the main current.' He withdrew his tender in return for a minority holding in Pullman Pacific, which then won the business without opposition.

Pullman had a shorter way with the host of lesser rivals with whom he contended, whether they were older-established than himself or had been drawn into the business by his own exemplary success. He would permit them, without interference, to complete their designs, procure their patents, construct their prototypes and even win a contract or two with lesser railroads. Then he moved in on them, employing one or another of the established strategies of robber barons of the period. He would undercut them into bankruptcy, and then buy their goodwill and patents for a knock-down price. Alternatively, as their first cars were about to enter service he would file a trumped-up law suit on spurious grounds of patent-infringement. Having procured an injunction against the use of the cars concerned, his lawyers moved repeatedly for adjournments of the case for the assembly of essential evidence – and the little rival would go bust in the meantime. At his most charitable, and as circumstances increasingly permitted him, he bought out the more stubborn competitors at prices they found hard to refuse.

Thus Pullman rapidly became the uncrowned but unquestioned king of American trains. The passengers may have suffered, as this church-going millionaire hypocrite ensured his workers did when business underwent the mildest recession. But if Carnegie had to make way to Pullman's monopoly, as he did, there was nobody in America who could, or at least effectively did, otherwise.

An early Union Pacific train featuring Pullman Palace Cars.

3. La Compagnie Internationale

Disillusioned by Pullman's phoney luxury though he was, Georges Nagelmackers returned to Europe at the end of 1868 with the inspiration that was to make international rail travel a reality for the first time.

He had noted that Pullman's otherwise lamentable monopoly had had one strongly beneficial effect – the practice of 'through-running'. Before, when a traveller undertaking a long journey came to the end of one railroad company's line, which he frequently did after only a few hours, he had to dismount from the ·train and board another. The time wasted and the in-convenience caused were sufficient in themselves to deter any-one from travelling round the country for pleasure. Merely to go from New York to Chicago necessitated five such changes, two or three of them, as a rule, in the middle of the night, and some scarcely less modest trips involved over a dozen.

As Pullman had contracts with most major railroad companies he was able to engineer a radical change – it was now the car that changed trains, with the passengers remaining on board. Nagelmackers's scheme was to extend the concept to complete trains, with only the locomotive being changed at each com-pany's terminus.

He conceived that the trains would be owned and operated by an enterprise independent of the railway companies them-selves, moving freely not only across their boundaries but across national ones as well, in the course of a single journey.

Looking back, it may seem remarkable that no such trains existed already. European railways were well developed by the late 1860s. After long procrastination, partly because the railway was a British invention, continental countries had (at about the time of Nagelmackers's birth) belatedly caught railway mania – that epidemic of the nineteenth century, through which poten-tial investors from shopkeepers to governments handed over their money almost at the mention of the word 'railway', without inquiring into a line's commercial prospects.

France had led the way, closely followed by Prussia. Nagel-mackers's native Belgium became the proud possessor of one of the most over-intensive networks. Backward Spain caught the disease and invested heavily in railways for which the country then had little use; the fervour was such that when a Madrid newspaper accused Maria Christina, the Queen Mother, of trying surreptitiously to water railway stock, her palace was mobbed by shareholders who chased her across the border into exile – though the shares appear to have been almost worthless in any event. Even Holy Russia embraced this instant symbol of progress, the Tsar entrusting the development of railways to his son and heir, the Tsarevitch Nicholas. Thus the latter made his first and, as later events were to prove, thoroughly character-istic contribution to his country's history. Presented by the American surveyors who had been called in to plan the first line,

OPPOSITE The cover of *The Continental Traveller*, a journal launched by Nagelmackers to promote international rail travel.

Nagelmackers during a visit to Russia in 1888. His business dealings with Tsarevitch Nicolas were unprofitable but culminated in the Trans-Siberian Express

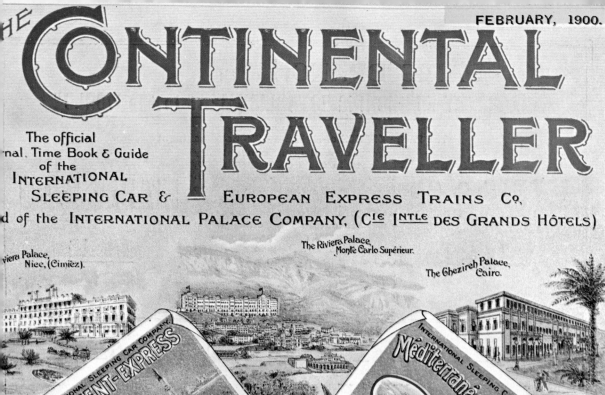

FEBRUARY, 1900.

THE CONTINENTAL TRAVELLER

The official
Journal, Time Book & Guide
of the
INTERNATIONAL
SLEEPING CAR & EUROPEAN EXPRESS TRAINS Co.
and of the INTERNATIONAL PALACE COMPANY, (Cⁱᵉ Iⁿᵗˡᵉ DES GRANDS HÔTELS)

The Riviera Palace, Monte Carlo Supérieur.

Riviera Palace, Nice, (Cimiez).

The Ghezireh Palace, Cairo.

Palace, Lisbon.

INTERNATIONAL SLEEPING CAR COMPANY
ORIENT-EXPRESS

FOR PARIS, BUDA-PEST, BELGRADE, VIENNA, AND CONSTANTINOPLE

INTERNATIONAL SLEEPING CAR COMPANY
Méditerranée-Express
LONDON to The RIVIERA. THREE TIMES WEEKLY
NICE MONTE-CARLO, MENTONE

Château Royal, d'Ardenne.

OSTEND-VIENNA-TRIESTE EXPRESS.

COMPAGNIE INTERNATIONALE DES WAGONS-LITS
SUD-EXPRESS
BIARRITZ, SAN SEBASTIAN, VALLADOLID
MADRID LISBON AND GIBRALTAR

LUCHON-EXPRESS
Train de Luxe direct

Therapia Palace, on the Bosphorus.

Elysée Palace Hotel, Paris.

Palace, Constantinople.

Published Monthly, at the London Offices of the Company, 14, Cockspur Street, S.W.

COMP.ⁱᵉ INTERNATIONALE DES WAGONS-LITS
& DES GRANDS EXPRESS EUROPÉENS

TRAINS DE LUXE :

Ostende-Vienne-Express
tous les jours.

Ostende-Carlsbad-Express
tous les jours (en été).

Ostende-Constantza-Express
hebdomadaire.

Ostende-Trieste-Express
hebdomadaire.

NORD-EXPRESS

Tous les jours entre :

Ostende et Berlin

Deux fois par semaine entre :

Ostende-Saint-Petersbourg
et
Paris-Saint-Petersbourg

WAGONS-LITS :

Ostende-Cologne

Ostende-Bâle

Ostende-Paris

WAGONS-RESTAURANTS :

Bruxelles-Paris

Bruxelles-Verviers

Bruxelles-Bâle

Herbesthal-Jeumont

WAGONS-SALONS :

Bruxelles-Paris

Bruxelles-Verviers

AGENCES DE LA COMPAGNIE

Bruxelles : Agence Principale à la Gare du Nord.
Sous Agences : à l'Hôtel Belle-Vue; au Grand Hôtel; à l'Office Central, rue de l'Écuyer, 65-67.

Ostende : Pavillon Wagons-Lits, à côté du Kursaal.
Liége : chez M. Crahay, libraire, rue de l'Université.

En HOLLANDE :
Amsterdam : chez MM. Lissone et Zoon, Singel, 155.

from St Petersburg to Moscow, he pulled the map showing its meandering course towards him, picked up a ruler and a pen and drew a straight line between the two cities, declaring: 'This, gentlemen, will be your route.'

They protested that it would miss all the intervening towns which they had so painstakingly linked. 'So', he replied, 'let the towns come to the railway.' And with absurd and immeasurably costly economic consequences, it was done.

By the time of Nagelmackers's return to Europe eighty thousand miles of lines were already in use, crisscrossing the whole continent from the Russian capital to Lisbon, and from Aberdeen in Scotland to Bucharest in Rumania. But the various railway companies and administrations viewed one another with distrust and hostility. They guarded their territorial exclusivities with obsessional jealousy; and for a coach, let alone a whole train, belonging to one company to pass over another's lines was almost unthinkable and virtually never permitted, unless a royal personage or a prominent statesman were aboard. Another company's rolling stock might be inferior, which would alienate passengers; or it might be superior, and so lure away their custom. In any event a loss of prestige might be involved. And what means were there of guaranteeing that the other company would not falsify traffic returns to cheat on paying over a proper share of the revenue?

Furthermore, nationalistic feelings were running high. What patriotic German would tolerate the presence of a French train in anywhere but France, for example, let alone ride in one, and vice versa?

Nagelmackers was convinced that he had found the solution to this impasse. As Belgium was a neutral country so his enter-

OPPOSITE A Wagons-Lits poster advertising the Train Bleu.

One of the first locomotives to pull Nagelmackers's opulent carriages.

prise would be a neutral, non-nationalistic one and no feelings of territorial encroachment could arise.

He would provide the trains free of any charge to the railway companies, who would none the less be entitled to levy a full fare from each passenger carried, in return only for granting the use of their lines and providing a locomotive. Nagelmackers would cover his outlay and make his profit by surcharging travellers for the extra convenience and luxury he offered; and having seen how willing Americans were to pay as much as

Leopold II, King of All the Belgians, and, it was unkindly added, Man of all the Money. He lent his name to the list of subscribers to La Compagnie Internationale in exchange for continuing overdraft facilities at Nagelmackers's family bank.

OPPOSITE A 1909 poster advertising P & O Lines. Nagelmackers persuaded the company to divert their ships to Brindisi to meet his trains from London and to lend their name to the express, which shortened the journey to India by several days.

three or four dollars a day for the very minor advantage of travelling in a Pullman 'palace', he had no doubt that people would flock to ride on his *trains de luxe*.

Returning to Liège, Georges put his proposal before his father. Whatever the reservations the latter may have had about the practical viability of the venture, he was financially as well placed to indulge a son's entrepreneurial fancies as he had been to pay for a year and a half's sojourn in the United States, in which to recover from love-sickness.

Word was passed to King Leopold, who readily agreed that his name be placed on the list of subscribing shareholders, on the sole condition, it seems, that he did not actually have to pay over any money. He also gave young Georges a fulsome letter of introduction 'To Whom It May Concern'. Thus armed, Georges set off to launch his first immodest enterprise: a luxury express service from Paris to Berlin.

As part of their preparations for war with one another, both France and Germany were then eager to curry Belgium's favour and ease her out of her neutrality. It was a bizarre outcome of these diplomatic manoeuvrings that both countries readily conceded to the royally backed Belgian proposal to operate a train between their two capitals.

No sooner had the ink dried on the necessary protocols than Nagelmackers, financed by his now impressed father, commissioned five carriages from a coachbuilder in Vienna. They were surely the world's finest at the time. Each was divided into three compartments, containing four plush armchairs apiece, with backs that folded down at night so that mattresses could be placed upon them by the attendant, who could then make them up into beds. Not only were they more comfortable than Pullman's, they provided greater privacy – by paying for two railway fares and four surcharges, a proposition within the means of many, a traveller could have a whole compartment to himself.

At the beginning of July 1870 the carriages were ready to go into service. On the thirteenth of that month the French Ambassador was granted an interview with the King of Prussia, and reported the proceedings to his government by telegram. This message, the famous 'Ems telegram', was intercepted by Bismarck, who doctored it in such a way as to make it appear that extreme insults had been exchanged. France declared war on 19 July.

That was, needless to say, the end of the Paris–Berlin Express for the time being. But the war – and Nagelmackers seems to have been one of the exceptionally few who failed to predict it – brought with it a new opportunity. For more than a decade Britons had been by far the most numerous international travellers on the continent of Europe, passing between Calais and Trieste on their way east, boarding a Peninsular and Orient steamer in the latter port. Many of them were army officers,

RIGHT The arrival of the P & O Bombay Express at Marseilles, 1913.

BELOW The Belgian headquarters of La Compagnie Internationale, 1883.

colonial officials, tea planters and the like going to serve the Queen-Empress in India and Burma. They were joined by increasing numbers of tourists being dispatched by Mr Thomas Cook and Messrs Dean and Dawson to Egypt and the Holy Land.

The trip overland across Europe, rather than by sea from Southampton, was extremely popular, not only because it cut several days off the journey time, but also because it circumvented the Bay of Biscay, to whose notoriety a host of manufacturers of patent but useless anti-seasickness preparations were indebted for their fortunes. Now the railway went through a battlefield, and the service was disrupted.

Nagelmackers stepped smartly into the breach. He quickly devised an alternative route through Italy, ending in Brindisi, and signed the necessary contracts with the railway companies involved with little delay or opposition. He approached the P & O Line, who were only too ready to lend their name to the proposed train, which was baptized 'The P & O Express', and to divert their ships to Brindisi for the voyage to Alexandria and Bombay.

The type of passenger was not, perhaps, that which Nagelmackers had originally had in mind. G.W.Stevens, a Victorian travel writer, took the train and described the passengers with entirely unintentional irony:

'There was not a single passenger who was not a Briton, and their trade was not difficult to see. Fair-haired and blue-eyed, square-shouldered and square-jawed, with puckered brows and steadfast eyes that seemed to look outwards and inwards at the same time, self-contained, self-controlled and self-reliant, they were unmistakable builders – British Empire builders.

'The faces of the women were serene with the serenity of those who have seen too many strange sights to be surprised now at anything; and in their patient aspect, there was a hint of the tragic heroism that sends its children to be brought up by strangers and forget their mothers.

'The Empire builders were going forth to their long work again. This man was going to his collectorship in the Central Provinces, that to his tea plantation in Assam. . . . The ruddy subaltern was going out to have a shot for the Gippy army.

'The Imperial Englishman talks little, though there is a freemasonry about the smoking room which melts down a great part of his native reserve. When he does talk, it is not of money, like the travelling American, nor of beer and timetables like the travelling German, but of sport. The foreigner in like case makes talking his main business; the Englishman appears to throw out his talk as a kind of afterthought and accompaniment to smoking. On the cloud of tobacco floats occasionally a brief reminiscence of many woodcock, or a hint to the young pig-sticker.

'Remember, this train leaves London every Friday night,

and its freight is always the same. [It] is a very vital link in that band of scarlet that grips the world.'

Business was brisk and before long it was necessary to book oneself a place on board the weekly train from Ostend to Brindisi more than a month in advance. The operation quickly became profitable and Nagelmackers, provided with further finance by his delighted father, went into a joint venture with P & O and built a hotel in Brindisi, one of the best in Europe, where passengers might await the boat in comfort. That, too, prospered; a further five carriages were built and the train's frequency was doubled to twice a week.

Then the war ended. The French, in the meantime, had tunnelled through the Alps under Mont Cenis, providing a much shorter and faster railway connection between the English Channel and the Mediterranean than Nagelmackers's route – and they saw no reason to allow Nagelmackers to run his trains through it, preferring to keep the revenue from the British Empire builders and excursionists to the Middle East to themselves.

The Peninsular and Orient's board promptly ditched the Belgian and signed with the French; and Nagelmackers was left with ten idle carriages, a half share in a now little-patronized hotel and an extremely sceptical father. Perhaps to keep his spirits up, and to lend his enterprise an air of plausibility it was so remarkably lacking, he registered it as a company for the first time, under the grand name of La Compagnie Internationale des Wagons-Lits. After a pause for thought, he added the still more imposing words 'et Grands Express Européens'.

The truth behind the façade was unedifying. He touted his wares – the two finest trains in Europe – across the continent, and found no takers. In the absence of diplomatic advantage or the contingencies of war not a single company was willing to replace its own rolling stock with that of Nagelmackers. Apparently in order to rid themselves of his persistence and to demonstrate to him his wrong-thinking, two French companies reluctantly agreed to attach one or another of his carriages to existing trains, in which passengers might travel for a surcharge. The contracts were cancellable by the railway companies at any moment, without notice. The expenses of the operation from Nagelmackers's side were so impractical that he had to impose severe surcharges. As a result his income averaged that from a single passenger for every two runs of one of his opulent coaches.

His father, while refraining from driving his son into bankruptcy, was not inclined to indulge him further, and the career of La Compagnie Internationale seemed to be near its end.

OVERLAND TICKE
ATLANTIC &

OVERLAND
TICKET
AND
FREIGHT
OFFICE.
THROUGH RATES
TO
ALL POINT
EAST
EAMSHIP TICK
TO
NCIPAL CIT
OF
EUROP

4
ATLANTIC
&
Pacific R.R.
ATCHISON,
TOPEKA &
SANTA FÉ R.R.
—
St. LOUIS &
SAN FRANCISCO R
JOHN L. TRUSLOW.

No. 4
OVERLAND
PASSENGER OFFICE

TICKETS TO
ALL POINTS EAST.

4. Enter Colonel Mann

A manifestation of the American railway boom, on board which Colonel Mann tried to climb too late.

It was at this moment, the nadir of Nagelmackers's fortunes, that Colonel William d'Alton Mann, recently of the United States Cavalry, galloped, as it were, to the rescue, in the unlikely guise of a 'boudoir car' salesman.

To say that Colonel Mann was a rogue and a confidence trickster with redeeming features, which he was, calls for some not unentertaining exploration into his past, if his entry into the business of international rail travel is to be understood.

Mann was Nagelmackers's senior by six years and had been brought up as the youngest of a farmer's five children in Perkins Township, Ohio. At the age of eighteen he had married for the first of several times, and gone to Oberlin College to study civil engineering. His stay at university lasted only a few weeks – he claimed later that this was because he had promptly answered the call to arms at the outbreak of the American Civil War. In fact between his leaving and his signing with the Union Army there was an intervening period of almost a year, which he had reasons to gloss over, as he did with so many events in his life.

He departed from Oberlin on receiving sudden news that an uncle had left him an inn in Grafton, Ohio, and decided without hesitation that he would rather own and run a business than undergo the arduous process of acquiring a profession. Apparently having given his bride the slip, he arrived in Grafton to find the inn derelict. Undaunted, he persuaded a local builder and craftsmen to repair it on credit, the understanding being that he would repay them as soon as the first customers arrived and the revenue started to flow in.

The inn was restored. Customers began to arrive; but somehow the money failed to find itself in the hands of the builder and the craftsmen. When they became, in his view, overpressing, he disappeared one night across the state border into Michigan. There, in Detroit, he completed his vanishing act by volunteering for military service, smooth-talking his way into an immediate commission as captain in the cavalry. Having spent much of his boyhood on horseback, he was an extremely accomplished equestrian, and he was quickly sent east to serve in the area of Washington, arriving there in the summer of 1861, when the Union cause was at a low ebb.

'Whoever heard of a dead cavalryman?' General Hooker acidly remarked; and it was the case that a commission in a mounted regiment was regarded rightly as a soft option. The cavalry then were rarely to be found near the front lines, acting mostly in the capacity of messengers and couriers. Mann, in his idiosyncratic way, did a great deal to improve upon that reputation and win for the United States Cavalry a name for bravery – indeed bravado – and valour on the battlefield.

Having taken part in the fiasco of the Battle of Bull Run, he turned his mind to the problem being caused by the confederate General J.E.B. Stewart. With five thousand horsemen armed with sporting guns and fowling pieces he was marauding behind the Union lines, ambushing and looting with apparent impunity. Outnumbered ten to one by fifty thousand Union infantrymen who had been withdrawn from the front to capture him or, failing that, to chase him and his men back behind their own lines, they derailed supply trains, set fire to ammunition stores, attacked observation posts from the rear and ransacked army camps, and were never once apprehended.

As the cavalry was held in such disdain by the military commanders, Mann's sensible proposal that it was folly to try to use foot-soldiers to fight mounted commandos and that horsemen should be employed instead was ignored until he addressed the Secretary for War personally. The response was swift. At his own suggestion Mann was sent back to Detroit, where good horsemen were to be found, to recruit and organize cavalry brigades to go out into the field against Stewart's marauders.

Within a few weeks of his return he raised, equipped and dispatched the 5th Michigan Cavalry to the eastern front. He then formed two more, the 6th and 7th. Custer, having recently passed out from West Point last in his class, applied for the command of the latter, but he was passed over by the Governor in favour of Mann himself, who thus became, soon after his thirtieth birthday, the youngest colonel in the army.

By the time he arrived back in the east with his brigade, those whom he had sent on ahead had already met with considerable success. Indeed all that was left of Stewart's marauders was a force of less than a hundred men, many of them Confederate deserters who had been recaptured and offered the option of becoming commandos or going to the stockade, under Colonel John Mosby. Mann claimed as his due the honour of wiping them out.

It cannot be said that he acquitted himself with distinction. Indeed his approach to the task was later to become thoroughly reminiscent of his business tactics: slapdash reconnaissance followed by a headlong charge.

A report reached him that Mosby's troop had been sighted near Kettle Run, and he went there with his men and set up camp by the side of the railroad track – about the most exposed and easily attacked site he could have found. On five successive days he sent out as many parties of mounted scouts to establish Mosby's whereabouts. Had he sent them out on foot they might have moved about quietly enough to find their prey. As it was, Mosby's men, although encumbered by a clumsy artillery piece, had little difficulty in dodging their searchers and went unseen.

At nightfall on the fifth day Mosby and his troop crept near to Mann's camp and bedded down on a timbered hillside overlooking it and the railroad. Next morning they awakened to the sound of Mann's bugle calling reveille. They walked down the hill to the track, removed a rail, cut the telegraph wires and withdrew. Minutes later a twelve-car supply train came down the line and overturned. Mosby took careful aim with his howitzer from the top of the hill and fired two shots straight into the boiler of the locomotive, which exploded. His men wandered down to collect the loot. Finding a consignment of fresh shad packed in ice, they lit a barbecue by the side of the track and cooked and consumed the fish before retiring.

Almost incredibly, it took Mann's cavalry all that time to put on their uniforms, breakfast and saddle and mount their horses, before going to investigate the cause of the explosion. They arrived while the last of Mosby's men were straggling, stomachs full, back to their hilly retreat.

It seems that without even considering the advisability of deploying his men round the hill and attacking from all sides, Mann massed them together, grouped them into columns of four and led them galloping up a narrow lane in a single, frontal charge. Mosby drove back the first two waves of attack with his howitzer before he ran out of ammunition and withdrew discreetly down the other side of the hill to raid again another day.

'We whipped him like the devil,' Mann reported to his general. In fact, while it was true that Mosby had had to leave his artillery piece behind, his side's account of the losses was one killed and four wounded. The 7th Michigan under Mann lost four men killed, fifteen wounded and an unreported number of horse casualties.

Fortunately for Mann, there was little leisure time in Washington for post-mortems into minor débâcles. The two sides were now preparing for the Battle of Gettysburg, and he was placed under the command of Custer who, one year his junior, had now become a general.

On 3 July, at Rommel's Farm, Custer ordered Mann and his troops into battle with the cry of 'Come on, you wolverines!'. In his official report he wrote later: 'Colonel Mann is entitled to much credit', and he quoted an account given him by one of Mann's lieutenants: 'For minutes which seemed like hours, amid the clashing of sabres, the rattle of small-arms, the agonised deprecations, the demands to surrender, the undaunted replies and the pleas for mercy, the Confederate column stood its ground.' To be precise, they killed a quarter of Mann's brigade of four hundred men in less than fifteen minutes, before he ordered a retreat.

It was the last action Mann was to see. Apparently under something of a cloud, although for reasons that have become lost as a result of his energetic covering of his own tracks, he spent the remaining days of his military service in an army camp, secretively devising 'improvements in the design of the accountrements of cavalrymen' and procuring patents on them.

Have procured these, he resigned his commission and spent

a couple of months touring cavalry units, exploiting to the utmost bonds of comradeship-in-arms in order to procure testimonials for his 'accountrements' from various officers. He then sold the designs for a handsome sum to the Department of War; given that he had devised them while he was still in the army, they were probably state property in any case.

With money in his pocket, he blithely returned to Grafton to apologize to his creditors for his swift disappearance, explain to them that it had been necessitated by an onrush of patriotic fervour and pay them off. No hint of conscience accompanied his gesture. Quite simply, a new plan had formed in his mind – this time to defraud the public rather than the government – and to carry it out he had need of an unencumbered title to property.

The United States was in the grip of oil fever. The Rockefeller fortune, spouting from the ground in the form of liquid gold, was already legendary, and the middle classes were clamouring for an opportunity to stake a claim in the new wealth. Reading through newspapers of the period one encounters pages and pages of advertisements, a few of them possibly genuine but most of them facile frauds, offering the public the privilege of investing their savings in new oil finds. Even a journal as respectable as the *New York Tribune*, which should have been less careless of its readers' welfare, was crammed with absurd offers of monthly dividends of 25 cents per share on one-dollar shares – the first dividend payable immediately upon receipt of the investment.

The way the confidence trick was worked was simple enough: the first suckers to send in their money were scrupulously paid their 'dividends' and the remainder of the money was promptly invested not in oil fields but more advertisements; the suckers were able to show their friends and acquaintances positive and irrefutable evidence that the advertisements were genuine, and

One of the results of America's oil fever: an oil creek, 1865. One of Colonel Mann's first confidence tricks was to sell shares in land which he fraudulently declared had the 'black gold'.

LEFT The heading of a 'Special Time Table' in honour of a VIP traveller.

BELOW LEFT The Wagner cars became fierce competitors to Pullman's cars and were regarded by travellers as being more comfortable.

RIGHT Pictorial railway ticket from *America Revisited*.

RAWING ROOM CARS.

Through Between

LAYTON,

R DELAY!

E NEW FAST TRAIN.

any to Clayton.

train leaving Saratoga 8.10 a. m. Leaves
4.05 p. m.; Round Island Park, 4.15 p. m.;
ter Park, 5.15 p. m. Passengers for Water-
tawa and Ogdensburg take through coach
at Utica : 10 minutes for Lunch at Lowville

PRESS.

yton to Albany.

eaving Alexandria Bay. 7.30 a. m.; West-
d Park, 8.20 a. m. Leaves Ogdensburg, 7.40
Car at Theresa Junction 9.38 a. m., without
at Carthage 10.25 a. m. Lunch at Lowville
enectady with train arriving Saratoga 6.05 p. m.
g Room Car from Utica, 5.50 p. m. arrives

more money poured in, to be partially reinvested in still more and larger advertisements. And so on it went until the promoters eventually received a batch of remittances sufficiently large for it to be worth their while to grab the money and run.

It had occurred to Mann that with the bequest of the inn had come one hundred acres of apparently useless land, which might now be put to a purpose. It also occurred to him that he had no need to go to the expense of advertising in the press – his old comrades-in-arms were about to receive their mustering-out money. Before he left Grafton he bought an option on a further two hundred acres near his own plot for forty-five dollars. And on his way back east he spent considerably more on a single acre near a genuine oilfield in Pennsylvania itself. He then went to New York and registered the United Service Petroleum and Mining Company.

His choice of name was shrewder than it at first appeared. For it was not, by the regulations of the time, such as to provoke any objection from the registrar. But once having received permission to use it, he promptly contracted it on his letter headings to 'The US Petroleum and Mining Company'.

He persuaded a prominent cavalry general with whom he had been at Gettysburg, Winfield Scott Hancock, not only to agree to become the company's president but, such was his fervour, to invest $1,000 of his own money in the concern. He then drew up one of the most blatantly dishonest prospectuses in the history of fraudulent American oil companies – which was, of course, a considerable achievement.

A reading of the prospectus shows that Mann lacked the necessary foresight to devise a truly successful fraud. With what was to prove fatal abandon, he declared in his eagerness to get the money in fast: 'Successful drilling will be completed within sixty days. There is no possibility of loss. The reputation of all concerned makes this certain.' He added: 'Persons in the Army can send Treasury notes, drafts, Government bonds, Post Office or Paymaster's Orders to our Office in New York.'

Having printed his prospectus, he went to a hardware store and purchased a small bottle of lubricating oil. He then went to Washington and installed himself in a suite in Owen's Hotel.

Afternoon after afternoon, he played host to groups of Union officers. His sales pitch, as recounted later in court, was of such breathtaking crudity that one wonders how the five brigadier-generals, twelve colonels and twenty-eight officers of lesser rank who fell for it could possibly have just won a war.

Taking the phial of lubricating oil (which, of course, bears no resemblance to crude) from his pocket, he would pass it round as a sample of what lay under the ground in Grafton. He would then let drop the intelligence that he was about to offer the public one hundred thousand shares at $3 dollars each; but because he was so overwhelmingly fond of the Union Army, he

OPPOSITE One of the attractive posters issued by La Compagnie Internationale.

SUMMER ON THE FRENCH RIVIERA
BY THE BLUE TRAIN

had felt compelled to give his old friends a chance to buy for a mere $1 a share.

One of the few who resisted his lure was General Custer, although Mann sent Mrs Custer a large bunch of flowers; but that may have been more on account of the General's antipathy towards Mann than of any business sense. The other officers paid over, between them, no less than $57,000 in the course of ten days.

The ten days ended on Palm Sunday. Colonel Mann took part in the Victory parade, marching at the head of the 7th Michigan, and then made a hasty tour of the paymasters' tents, pulling his rank to gain permission to leave a stack of prospectuses in each one. Over the next few hours he collected a further $1,700.

Of the total of $58,700 he transferred $45,000 into his own bank account, as payment for his land titles and options, at the same time omitting to transfer the latter into the company's name. He faked a telegram from Grafton, 'reporting' an oil strike on a plot of land adjoining his, which he proudly passed round at the next board meeting.

But the sixty days came and went, and then another sixty; and the major investors in the US Petroleum and Mining Company, still being in possession of no more oil than that in the Colonel's phial, became somewhat restless. A small group of them met and decided to go to Grafton to see for themselves what was happening.

Mann did not hear of what he called their 'contemptible subterfuge' until they were halfway there, but when he did he immediately sent a panicked telegram to the caretaker he had hired there, instructing him to hire labour, dig holes, beg and borrow machinery and explain that most of the equipment was away being repaired. But the game was up; a warrant was issued for Mann's arrest and after a night in goal he was released on $5,000 bail.

In court Mann was defended by the most renowned and redoubtable trial lawyer of the day, David Dudley Field. The case started in a blaze of newspaper publicity for the prosecution's entirely correct charge of fraud perpetrated against war veterans. But Field, employing every known obstructionist tactic and some previously unknown ones as well, managed to stretch out the trial for several months, despite his patent lack of an adequate defence. Eventually he succeeded in creating in the courtroom an atmosphere of such unrelieved and intolerable boredom that finally even the judge broke, and abruptly announced one morning that he had decided that the case fell outside his jurisdiction. He advised the litigants of their rights to sue under civil law. But they, too, had had enough, and in any case Mann, although still free, was no longer worth suing – all his ill-gotten money had been swallowed up by Field's fees.

OPPOSITE The casino at Monte Carlo. Its opening provoked storms of protest from Nice and other neighbouring French resorts where gambling was illegal.

73

With the brazenness that so often served him well Mann now repaired to Washington, represented himself as an unemployed war-hero and obtained an appointment as a tax collector in the defeated city of Mobile, Alabama, where he moved without procrastination.

Among his wide powers as a 'carpet-bagger' or 'reconstructionist' was that of sequestring property belonging to those who had fought for the Confederate cause. It was a power he employed energetically, both on the government's and on his own behalf, as is evidenced by the $4,700,000 he collected in this way for the United States in his first year of activity, and a further $5 million federal investigators were later to allege that he had pocketed.

So far from his being lynched, it did not take Mann long to establish himself as a thoroughly popular individual with Mobile's leading figures. This was simply explained by his fine sense of discrimination in deciding whose property to confiscate, and to whom to sell it at a bargain price on the government's behalf. The smaller men – storekeepers, farmers and the like – he treated ruthlessly. The cotton kings he levied lightly if Washington might otherwise become suspicious, but preferably not at all.

It would be hard to imagine a more flamboyant way for a civil servant to invest embezzled funds than that chosen by Colonel Mann. He bought up all four of Mobile's daily papers, merged them into one, entitled the *Register*, and dropped heavy hints that the wrath of the internal revenue collector would fall down hard on anyone who presumed to challenge his newly established press monopoly.

He promptly used his monopoly to present himself as candidate for election to the forty-first Congress, on the Democratic ticket. The main plank of his platform was hostility towards his own kind, carpet-baggers from the north, closely followed by opposition to rights for Negroes on the grounds of their mental inferiority.

After a husting during which four Negroes were killed for interrupting the Colonel's speech, Washington decided to send in agents to look into his affairs and the circumstances of his candidature. The evidence against him was not hard to find, and the federal authorities decided to intervene. They did so in the clumsiest possible way, by dispatching an official to Mobile to announce, the day before the polling took place, that Mann would be arrested and charged immediately afterwards with embezzling government money. But to cheat Washington was not exactly regarded as a heinous crime in the south, and if anything the intervention served to enhance Mann's local popularity.

The official was chased out of town, and in the early hours of the morning following election day Mann was declared returned to Congress by a sizeable majority. The declaration was something of a formality – the party Mann threw in the City Hall to celebrate his victory had begun several hours before.

But Washington had not given up yet, and in the week that followed a new set of investigators found several discrepancies in the poll. At some stations more votes had been recorded than the number of people who had come to vote. Some ballot boxes were unaccountably missing. Most remarkably of all, several Negro districts seemed, on the face of it, to have voted over-whelmingly for the racist candidate. A recount was held, and Mann's opponent was declared the victor.

His political career 'sabotaged by northern carpet-baggers', as he put it, Mann readdressed himself to the business of making money. For a newspaper proprietor in the south with few scruples, this was not an arduous task in those days. The people of the depressed and battered region had succumbed to railway mania as the answer to all their economic woes. No sooner had lines been built, they fondly imagined, than industry would spring up all the way along them, bringing untold wealth. As a result phoney railroad ventures, much like the fraudulent 'oil companies' of the north-east, were being launched on the public almost weekly.

Bent representatives in the state capital ensured the smooth passage of the bill of authorization for a new railroad that was never to be – and quite often a generous handout of public money as well (a percentage of which ended up in the pockets of the pliant senators). The role of the newspaper proprietor was to act as railroad promoter.

Mann began each promotion with a lengthy leading article of fulsome praise for the wisdom of the legislators who had authorized the project. This would be followed up, a few days later, with an advertisement making a public offer of stock, alongside a second article outlining the remarkable benefits the railroad would create and the extraordinary profits it would bring to its owners.

Of the money that poured in, Mann took one-fifth as his commission, passed another fifth to the legislators as theirs and gave the remainder to the company's directors. Follow-up reports would relate how great the progress was in the surveying work, and how imminent the start of actual construction was. More money came in. When the cow of public gullibility had been milked sufficiently, the company's officials disappeared.

The mania was so intense that despite repeated scandals, the money continued to flow – Mann successfully promoted some twenty such ventures in succession. The only one that went amiss was the one he launched on his own account. The disastrous error he made was to become so moved by the power of his own rhetoric as actually to try to construct the line.

The railroad was called the New Orleans, Mobile and

Chattanooga. The route was an engineer's nightmare, passing over swamps into which the track sank, and along beaches where it was swept away by the waves at high tide. After several reroutings it was completed by the end of 1870 at over double the projected expense, and it never showed a profit.

Mann paid off one major and particularly persistent contractor by handing him the ownership of the *Register*, which was of little further use to him anyway; and he left town shortly afterwards when a conveniently timed epidemic of yellow fever came near to Mobile.

The Colonel repaired to New York, and installed himself in a suite at the Astor House. Whether or not he cared much either way, his oil swindle of a few years previously had long been overshadowed by far grander ones that had followed in its wake, and it had been as good as forgotten.

He presented himself about town as Colonel Mann, civil engineer, Civil War veteran, newspaper proprietor and railroad director. And it was true that he was still bitten by the railroad bug.

It was not many weeks before Mann enlisted himself in the ranks of latter-day, would-be Pullmans – men who had seen what a success George Mortimer Pullman had achieved with his second-rate, or even third-rate, sleeping cars, and were confident that they could improve on them greatly.

They all made the same miscalculations. The first was that the railroad companies actually wanted to offer their customers the maximum comfort possible, when in reality they cared little and found Pullman's formula of providing the superficial illusion of luxury at far lower cost than true comfort a thoroughly satisfactory one. The second was to underestimate the lengths to which Pullman would go to use his now superior financial power to crush competition.

Pullman now owned a large manufacturing plant in Detroit, where a thousand employees were turning out over a hundred new cars a year, as well as repairing and refurbishing existing ones. The press had upgraded him from mere king of the business to being its 'Emperor Alexander', and he had no intention of permitting his position to be undermined by upstarts such as Colonel Mann.

Of all the rival cars that were designed and manufactured, Mann's was without doubt the most luxurious. Instead of the open plan, which Pullman espoused, he divided his coach into private compartments, in which passengers could be protected from one another's company, from snores at night and from the constant attentions of card sharps and patent-medicine and other pedlars. The armchairs were softly upholstered, the panelling more ornate than Pullman's, the carpets thicker. A lavatory was provided for every two compartments. Instead of

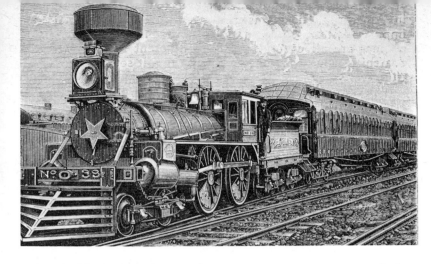

An American steam
engine and carriages,
1888.

a bunk-filled dormitory, the compartments converted into
sleeping quarters with four proper single beds.

A small railroad in New York State granted Mann a trial
contract to put his 'boudoir cars', as he called them, into service.
However welcome they were to passengers, the Pullman Company soon put a stop to the experiment by the simple means of
undercutting him out of the business. But even if Pullman had
made no move, the project was almost certainly doomed from
the start. So generous was Mann in allocating space that each
of his cars had places for only sixteen people. A Pullman car,
which was not much larger, could accommodate, if that is the
word for the conditions on board, three times as many. By
permitting more passengers to be crammed in, Pullman's open
cars meant more revenue for the railroad companies – and
comfort be damned.

To scrape together a few dollars the Colonel tried his hand at
the business of constructing private cars, then the prestige
symbols of the time. But he sold only one, and that by a combination of luck and ebullience.

It was his custom to breakfast each day at Delmonico's
Restaurant on a mutton chop, and to consume two bottles of
champagne at the bar before doing so. Standing there one
morning, working his way through the champagne, he over-
heard another customer discussing with a friend the agonizing
difficulties of finding a suitable birthday present for his lady
friend, a Miss Lily Langtry.

One by one humdrum gifts – diamond clusters, fur coats,
Fabergé eggs – were eliminated. Then Mann stepped boldly
forward and suggested that a private railroad car might be
appropriate. The deal was clinched for $100,000 before he sat
down to his chop; but it was the only one he ever sold.

He reasoned that if America had not time for his cars because
they were too luxurious, and if the Pullman monopoly was
unassailable anyway, he should move his business to another
place where Pullman did not exist and luxury was still in favour.
Taking two sample boudoir cars with him, he set sail for England.

77

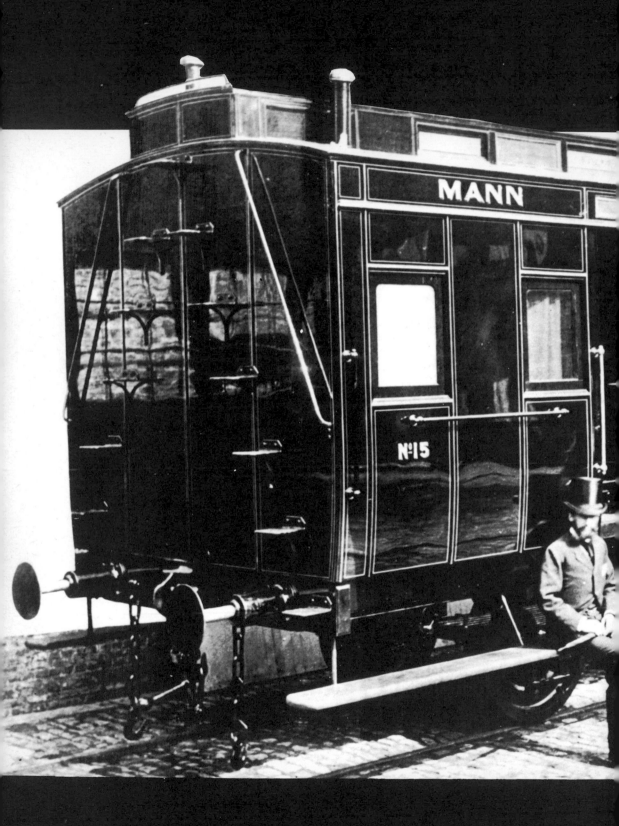

5. Exit Colonel Mann

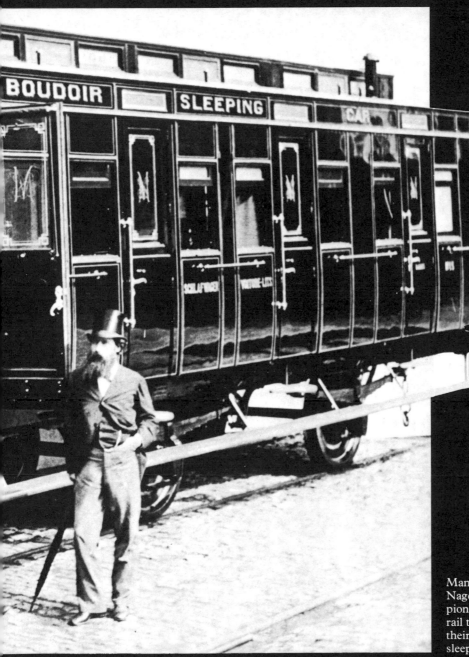

Mann and Nagelmackers, the two pioneers of international rail travel, showing off their pioneer Boudoir sleeping car.

Having parked his two boudoir cars in a siding, Colonel Mann installed himself in the Langham Hotel, London's unofficial headquarters for Americans who had espoused the Confederate cause. There he established his base camp from which to survey the European scene; and it did not take him long to learn of Nagelmackers's existence and activities.

At Mann's invitation, the two men met in London, the former trying to sell the latter a fleet of coaches. Nagelmackers admired them sincerely enough – they were certainly superior by far to his own rolling stock – but then confessed that he lacked the funds to pay for them. Mann promptly made an offer to go into partnership and to provide the necessary finance to relaunch La Compagnie Internationale. This offer was accepted.

There is some mystery as to Mann's sources of finance at this stage in his career. It seems unlikely that much of the fortune he had made swindling the United States Internal Revenue in Mobile had survived the débâcles of the New Orleans, Mobile and Chattanooga Railroad and his American sleeping-car business. It was rumoured much later that he had found an effective means of blackmailing members of the British aristocracy into subscribing shares. Certainly he claimed to have English backing for his venture; none of his alleged backers presented themselves as such in public, although it was still fashionable to be associated with railway enterprises; and he did not want for money.

If it is true that he supported himself and business through blackmail, one can only conjecture on the basis of circumstantial evidence as to how this came about. Later in life, after his return to New York, he was exposed by means of one of *Colliers* magazine's more persistent campaigns as an accomplished master of the art, counting Carnegies, Guggenheims and Rockefellers among his clients. The technique he employed was that of owning a social scandal sheet, writing items ostensibly for publication and soliciting gifts for their suppression. It was quite possible that it was in London that he developed this skill. By his own admission he cultivated the company of society journalists while he was there, and offered to subsidize at least two of them in setting up their own weekly publications. And it may have been that his entrée to the necessary information was facilitated by Lily Langtry, mistress of the Prince of Wales. One story was that he had tried to blackmail her on his arrival in England and that she somehow got the better of him – possibly by deflecting his blackmail energies.

Blackmail or not, he set himself up in business in grand style. He registered his concern under the name of the Mann Boudoir Sleeping Car Company in London, and in Oldham, Lancashire, acquired coachbuilding works with over 150 employees, whom he set to work without delay to produce boudoir cars. He then incorporated La Compagnie Internationale as a subsidiary of

The Prince of Wales –
subject of Colonel
Mann's notable
promotional coup when
HRH rode in a Mann
Boudoir Car to attend
the marriage of his
brother in St Petersburg.

his own company, suppressed the former's name and took over
from Nagelmackers as chief executive.

By then he knew the full details of Nagelmackers's failure to
establish a Pullman-like monopoly on the continent and
attributed his failing to what he saw as a European penchant for
deviousness, leading to gratification from making negotiations
as intricate and drawn out as possible, rather than moving in
fast and grabbing firm orders. He published an Anglo-French
prospectus in Paris, proclaiming that the company was now
under his 'general direction and personal supervision'. As soon
as new boudoir cars were completed in Oldham they were
shipped across the Channel and shown off to the directors of
railway companies; they were now made available to reporters,
who were invited to undertake journeys free of charge.

His most notable promotional coup was to persuade the
Prince of Wales – one presumes through the intercession of
Miss Langtry – to ride in a boudoir car from London to St
Petersburg to attend the marriage of his brother, the Duke of

OPPOSITE The sumptuous interior of a Wagons-Lits salon car, 1899.

Edinburgh, to Princess Marie of All the Russias. Immediately after the ceremony he travelled to St Petersburg himself to retrieve his carriage, and took the opportunity of giving a group of reporters a free ride home, a gesture for which he was handsomely repaid in their glowing and prominently published accounts.

Needless to say, among the most avid followers of Mann's publicity drive in Europe was George Pullman. So far he had been preoccupied with building up his monopoly in the United States; but that was now well entrenched, and the idea of allowing the potentially huge European market to fall to a puny competitor, whom he had so easily ousted from the domestic market, was anathema.

He therefore dispatched emissaries to London. The British Pullman Car Company was founded and English directors were appointed to run it.

They began boldly enough by announcing in *The Times* that contracts had been signed that would make 'Pullman Hotel Cars' available 'throughout the whole of Europe'. There was no truth whatever in the claim, which seems to have been designed partly to impress upon the boards of British and continental railways that there was but one established sleeping-car company on earth, and that was Pullman's.

The opening shot was followed up by the establishment of a car-building plant in Turin in Italy. While the company's labour relations were beginning to sour back home, the enthusiasm of the Italian workers who were hired for the new factory seems to have known few bounds, if the following address to Pullman and his chief of European operations, a Mr Rapp, is any guide:

TO

PULLMAN ESQUIRE, THE GREAT INVENTOR

OF THE

SALOON COMFORTABLE CARRIAGES

AND

MASTER RAPP, THE CIVIL ENGINEER,

DIRECTOR OF THE MANUFACTURE OF THE SAME

THE

ITALIAN WORKERS BEG TO UMILIATE

Welcome, welcome, Master Pullman,
The great Inventor of the Saloon Carriages.
Italy will be thankful to the man
For now, and ever, for ages and ages.

To Master Rapp we men are thankful
Cause of his kindness and adviser sages.
Our hearts of true gladness is full:
And we shall remember him for ages.

Should Master Pullman ever succeed
To continue is work in Italy [*sic*]
What we wish to him indeed
We hope to be chosen
To finish the work and work as a man
To show our gratitude to Master Pullman

– Fino and his friends

To Mann's not inconsiderable satisfaction, it wasn't long before Fino and his friends were being laid off. The Pullman Company signed, in the event, no more than two contracts to supply sleeping cars in Central Italy, and one contract for day coaches with the Midland Railway of England.

Mann engineered Pullman's defeat by spreading the idea that open-plan coaches were conducive to licentiousness and debauchery. To the director-generals of railway companies he painted a vivid picture of life on board Pullman cars in America, with respectable women being importuned by strangers as they lay helpless in their beds, of unmarried couples bedding down in public and the like. One of his favourite tales was of a group of English ladies visiting Canada. Shown to their berths in a Pullman car by the conductor, they expressed their amazed displeasure that they were not given a private compartment. The conductor assured them that ninety-seven per cent of women passengers found no objection to the arrangement. 'Then I can only say that American women are ninety-seven per cent more immoral than I had imagined,' replied the leader of the group.

In truth, of course, if any arrangements were suited to licentiousness on board trains those Mann provided on his boudoir cars were; and for the price of four supplements a private bedroom could be obtained for oneself, with no questions asked. Indeed Mann boudoir cars were soon to become well known as places of assignation for illicit lovers. D.H.Lawrence even had Lady Chatterley deplore 'the atmosphere of vulgar depravity on board *trains de luxe*'. In due course the availability of private compartments led to the emergence of a new and specialized type of prostitute, who frequented the booking halls of railway stations, ready to relieve the tedium of a journey from, say, Paris to Lyons, for any gentlemen with the wherewithal. A lower class of tart worked the ceinture lines around Paris, along which sleeping cars were moved from the Gare du Nord to the Gare d'Orsay.

Despite the speciousness of Mann's approach, his campaign for 'decency' worked excellently. 'I am told that it is not rare in America to find two in a berth,' wrote M. Bandereli of France's Chemins de Fer du Nord to Colonel Gourand, Pullman's agent in Paris, icily rejecting his proposal that he should use Pullman sleeping cars. 'American families are not embarrassed to be in a

OPPOSITE A Wagons-Lits car of 1888. Colonel Mann stressed their 'decency' – passengers travelled in private compartments – and alleged that open plan cars were conducive to licentiousness.

sleeping car in the middle of twenty strangers. Our morals here have not attained to that degree of civilization.' He gave the contract to Mann.

More contracts followed. Soon Mann boudoir cars were running not only within France but from Paris to Cologne and Vienna, and from Vienna to Munich. But the business was coming in too slowly for Mann's taste. Besides he was tiring of Europe and Europeans, finding the way of doing business too correct and turpitudinous, and the society dull. He spent more and more of his time in the saloon of the Langham Hotel, nostalgically reminiscing about the Deep South with fellow-Americans. When Nagelmackers went to London to remonstrate with him severely about paying insufficient attention to the company's expansion, Mann offered to give him back the post of director-general. Nagelmackers accepted with alacrity.

It was a moment when the railway companies of Europe were belatedly but suddenly deciding, one after the other, that the age of the sleeping car had arrived. Nagelmackers's more urbane and polished approach paid off where Mann's impatient charging-bull tactics had not. Within two months of resuming control he had signed no less than sixteen new contracts, and a total of fifty-seven Mann boudoir cars were soon in service in England, France, Germany, Austria-Hungary and Rumania.

With the upsurge of business came a revival of interest and confidence from Nagelmackers's father and his Belgian fellow-bankers. A consortium was formed to regain control of the business. In return for the gift of a private car (of such opulence that it gave rise to cries of protest from Social Democrat politicians that this was the kind of thing that sparked off revolutions), Leopold II agreed to appear at the head of the list. An approach was made to Mann, who agreed to sell for the outrageously high price of $5 million.

Mann took his money and returned to New York. There he set up the American Mann Boudoir Sleeping Car Company, but it never prospered. In due course he sold out to Pullman and went into business as a publisher and editor of a scurrilous social weekly, *Town Topics*, making more, it seems, from the revenue he obtained by supressing items than from the sale of the journal itself.

Had he remained in Europe he would have seen Pullman's humiliation there completed. But that pleasure passed, along with the company, to Nagelmackers. Pullman had signed but four contracts in all, and one of those was on a trial basis, subject to cancellation by the railway company without notice. He sent an emissary to Nagelmackers to propose a merger of their interests in Europe, to be called La Compagnie Internationale des Wagons-Lits et Wagons-Salons; Pullman was to receive half the shares in return for his extremely dubious goodwill and assets. Nagelmackers showed him the door.

Not long after Pullman's contracts in central Italy lapsed, and he did not seek to renew them. This again was good news for Nagelmackers, as through them Pullman had effectively been able to block the path of a direct service from Calais to Brindisi. That obstacle now removed, Nagelmackers bought the Pullman works in Turin for a very modest price, and began ferrying the Empire builders on their way eastwards again.

The company reverted to its old and grand name of La Compagnie Internationale des Wagons-Lits et Grands Express Européens and the scene was now set for the realization of Nagelmackers's greatest dream: to operate not merely carriages attached to existing trains, but trains themselves.

END OF A COOK'S
VOYAGE. A Punch
cartoon (1879) illustrates
'infuriated and
overwrought tourists
"finish off" their
conductor, at once more
thankfully putting foot
on their native shore'.

6. Troubles of Travelling

The Orient Express was Nagelmackers's first major triumph. Although it was to be followed by others no less impressive, it captured the public imagination as no other train could, and it did so instantly. Indeed in a period when in the minds of most westerners the Orient began somewhere round Hungary, it was one of the undisputed wonders of its age.

Edmund About and Henri Opper de Blowitz, two of the literary passengers on board the first run, wrote entire books about it that went into several editions. Long before Agatha Christie, Graham Greene and Hollywood turned their attention to the train, an extensive literature already surrounded it, and the legend of its mystique, romance and atmosphere of intrigue on board was already firmly implanted.

Among the more extraordinary works to be written about it was Maurice Debroka's *La Madonne des Sleepings* – 'sleepings' being the term used by the French for what the English called 'wagons-lits' – a novelette that was translated into over twenty languages and sold millions of copies. His heroine was a Lady Jane Wyndham, daughter of a Scottish duke. Having received an *éducation sportive* at Salisbury College, she turned her talents to making men fall in love with her, and becoming bored by them. She was, it seems, a woman of some attraction – Debroka, who claimed to have written the work in lipstick, described her breasts as 'being like doves caught in a pink net' – but little patience with the opposite sex. The climax of the book came when she boarded the Orient Express, telling the lover she was about to abandon on the platform of the Gare de l'Est that, before the journey was over, she was determined to find 'the imbecile who will cater to my whims and ripen in my garden of Hesperides some golden apples'. Debroka wrote: 'She is the true feminine puzzle.' But the only puzzle about her (apart from where she had acquired some contemptuous manners) was whether or not she got her imbecile – Debroka coyly resorted to a row of dots . . . .

The popular image of a normal carriage on a normal run of the Orient Express would have contained at least a young English lord setting off on grand tour (and losing his virginity to a glamorous lady diamond thief of indeterminate nationality and a certain age); a couple of gold smugglers; a pair of spies employed by rival powers trying to subvert one another over the iced Bollinger; and a deposed Balkan politician posing as a tobacco merchant and fleeing for his life.

One story that persistently went the rounds was of a compartment containing two women and two men, one of the latter a diminutive and silent Belgian. As a train entered a tunnel the lights suddenly went out. There was a piercing scream; and when the train emerged into daylight there were only three people in the compartment – the Belgian had disappeared. His

King Boris III of Bulgaria, an enthusiastic but dangerous amateur train driver. He defied anyone to prevent him from driving the Orient Express across his own kingdom, putting passengers' lives in peril.

body was found some miles further back along the track, the inside lining of his jacket ripped out. The people who were with him when he was defenestrated all swore that they had never met him before, had not exchanged a single word with him during the journey and had neither felt nor heard anything except the single scream.

It is true that during its career at least two government agents – one an American military attaché – either jumped or were thrown to their deaths from the Orient Express. It is also true that one of Nagelmackers's constant worries was that political violence might break out on board among the cosmopolitan passengers – when the train was trapped by a snow drift in the Balkans for several days the first move of the *chef de brigade* was to make the passengers take an oath on the Bible forswearing political discussion of any kind.

Probably the train's most famous and eccentric regular customer was King Boris of Bulgaria, who was a keen amateur engine driver and wore white overalls designed and made for him by his Parisian tailor. As long as he just stood in the cab, which he did for hours at a time, observing the professional driver at work, all was well, and Nagelmackers was pleased to indulge him – he was, after all, the most frequent hirer of the train's private carriage, which cost the equivalent of twenty first-class tickets. But then he began to pull monarchical rank, and to insist on taking over the controls himself. He was a devotee of speed and lacked a grasp of what signals meant. La Compagnie

Internationale intervened, the King was firmly ordered to desist and drivers were told that the punishment for allowing him to enter the cab would be dismissal. Little daunted, Boris would sit in his private carriage until the train crossed the border into Bulgaria. Then he would alight, already garbed in his overalls, and defy anyone to stop him from driving a train across his own kingdom.

There was nothing the company could do, short of finding a means of by-passing Bulgaria altogether. On one occasion he stoked the furnace far too enthusiastically. The flame blew back into the cab, setting the fireman's clothing ablaze. While the latter fell screaming to his death by the side of the track, the King raced straight on, and on arrival in Sofia offered himself to the passengers for applause for having made the Orient Express arrive on time despite the accident.

OPPOSITE A Wagons-Lits sleeping compartment by day. LEFT One converted for night.

As the countries of eastern Europe improved their railways so the Orient Express became faster and more direct. The route was changed to a more southerly direction, through what is now Yugoslavia. For some time passengers had to travel for thirty miles between two unconnected lines in digilences, but that was considered preferable to the Danube crossing and the hair-raising embarkation at Varna. Finally the line all the way from western Europe to Constantinople was completed, and it was possible to go all the way in a single train.

To travel on the Orient Express was exorbitantly expensive when compared with other contemporary costs, at £58 a person, or a total of £160 for a couple with a servant. In those days the latter sum could rent one a substantial mansion in a good district of London for a year. Working-class families who earned that amount annually were reckoned to be comfortably off for their station; it was sufficient for a couple with three children to eat meat regularly, live in a terraced house, be adequately clothed and warm, own their own medium-quality furniture and take an annual holiday at the seaside.

Similarly, £58 was the price of a new carriage, fourteen hand-tailored worsted suits or a bottle of whisky a week for over seven years. And £44, the discounted servant's fare, was as much as most of them were paid over a period of twelve months. Almost a century later that was the price of a three-day stay in Istanbul, including a return flight from London.

But as Nagelmackers was aware, there was an immense amount of middle-class money about. Death duties had yet to sting the bourgeoisie and in a single year in Britain over four thousand people inherited estates worth £19 million or more. Income tax was nominal. The numbers of people who could afford to employ servants had doubled in the past two decades. Over a million families had princely incomes of over £700 a year.

The rise of the newly rich spawned by the industrial revolution was a phenomenon that Thomas Cook had done surprisingly little to exploit. So long as Cook, a generation older than Nagelmackers, was alive and active, his firm's tours were more in the nature of educative excursions than holidays. They were, by comparison, inexpensive – a lengthy visit to Egypt and Palestine could cost less than a single journey on board the Orient Express. But Cook was no great believer in creature comforts – his customers were obliged to live in tents while visiting the Holy Land. And the aura of teetotalism, hymns and extemporized prayers after supper and the passing round of a plate for donations for the poor, which Cook would then hand over as though he had given the money himself, was a persistent one. For the prosperous middle class, Cook was the person to whom you entrusted your daughter on a guided trip abroad, rather than patronizing him yourself.

OPPOSITE Thomas Cook, the first 'package tour' operator, who provided excursions throughout the world with a routine of prayer and teetotalism.

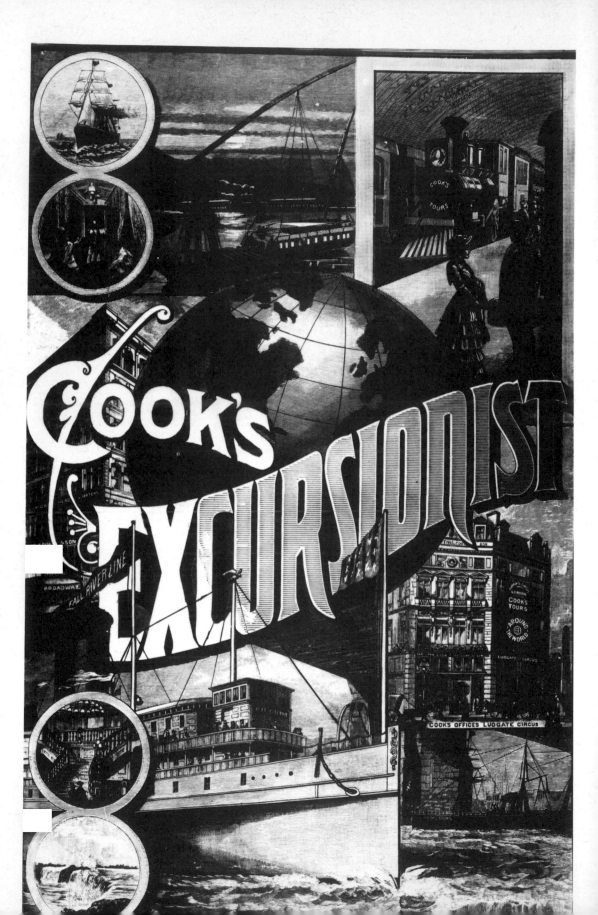

Cook's travellers in the Holy Land in front of their camp site. Cook offered early travellers distance rather than comfort.

No Puritan, Nagelmackers was in the business of offering luxury and enjoyment. The standards of comfort, service and food on board the Orient Express were, as I have mentioned, far superior to those available in all but a handful of grand hotels; even his provision of towels and soap for passengers was regarded as an innovation almost unknown before.

He had gauged the mood of the middle class – particularly the British and the German middle class – correctly. People flocked to board the Orient Express, mainly to enjoy its opulence and to say that they had been on it, in ever-increasing numbers. The frequency of the service increased, as did the number of available routes to Istanbul. The train gradually became more and more luxurious – bell-pushes were placed in the compartments, enabling one to summons one's maid or valet from the servants' quarters instantly. The servants of La Compagnie Internationale were decked out in uniforms and wigs as though they were in Versailles at the time of Louis XVI. The menus became more elaborate, and a fully equipped bathroom was added to the amenities.

But for Nagelmackers it was a success story that rebounded, for a reason beyond his control. The reason was the lamentable condition of the destination, Constantinople. For once one had travelled on his magnificent express, where was one to stay and what was one to do on one's arrival, short of taking the train home again?

The train's urbane atmosphere and remarkable comforts served to emphasize the primitiveness of the Ottoman capital. It was a city for adventurers, and the new kind of traveller Nagelmackers was fostering was rather a tourist, and a wealthy one at that, who would be markedly unamused to find, as the pioneering journalists did, sheep roaming the lobby of his hotel, and who expected 'abroad' to meet his preconceived requirements. How lamentably Constantinople failed to do this in those days is vividly portrayed by George Bradshaw in his *Guide to Turkey*, which he wrote and published shortly before the Orient Express's inauguration.

The items that Bradshaw considered essential for a traveller to bring with him to Turkey included his own cutlery, teapot and condensed milk, a Deane and Adams revolver and a folding bath. He could find not a single hotel in the town that could be recommended. He said of Missiri's, the place where most English visitors stayed, that it had 'a desolate, sepulchral appearance; and there is a general gloom pervading the whole establishment. The only advantage to be gained by going there and paying 18s. a day is that you are sure to meet the greater part of the English tourists in Istanbul.' None of the other hotels fared any better from his account, and he counselled the visitor to inspect them all and to opt for the one he found the least objectionable. 'Having now made up your mind where to

OPPOSITE A 1901 advertisement for the Constanza Express, one of the Wagon-Lits trains across Europe to the new tourist destination of Constantinople.

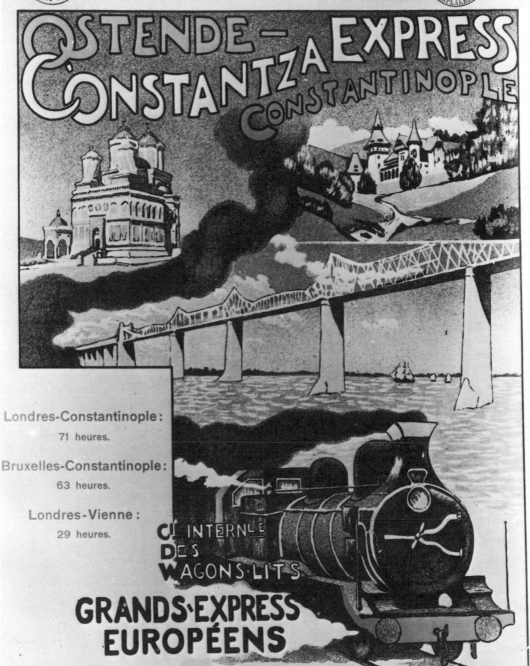

(Londres) - Ostende - Constantza - (Constantinople)

TOUS LES JOURS ENTRE:

(Londres) - Ostende et Vienne

OSTENDE - CONSTANTZA EXPRESS
CONSTANTINOPLE

Londres-Constantinople:

71 heures.

Bruxelles-Constantinople:

63 heures.

Londres-Vienne:

29 heures.

Cⁱᵉ INTERNⁱᵉ DES WAGONS-LITS

GRANDS EXPRESS EUROPÉENS

Imp. J.-E. Goossens, Bruxelles-Lille-Paris

Voie nouvelle la plus économique pour Constantinople

Pour tous renseignements et places à réserver, prière de s'adresser aux Agences suivantes de la COMPAGNIE INTERNATIONALE DES WAGONS-LITS et des GRANDS EXPRESS EUROPÉENS:

BRUXELLES: Agence principale à la Gare du Nord.
Sous-Agences: à l'*Hôtel Belle-Vue*.

OSTENDE: Pavillon Wagons-Lits à côté du Kursaal.
LIÈGE: chez M. CRAHAY, libraire, rue de l'Université.

go,' he continued gloomily, 'choose one of the numerous touters who are clamouring around you and give yourself up to him!'

He said that the restaurants 'are notorious for their rich, oily dishes', but singled out for commendation pickled pepper pods, 'ten times better than soda water for the cure of seediness and general disgust of human nature'. This appeared to be a common condition among English tourists. The whole place, he asserted,

'. . . swarms with Greek *klephti* (thieves) and Maltees, who are born for the express purpose of thieving. . . . Turkey being a free country, all the scum of Greece which is too bad even for the Hellenes themselves to tolerate, which is saying a great deal, seeks refuge in the land of onions and garlic, and fatten on the strangers in the land. . . . [When staying in a hotel] there are certain advantages in leaving one's door unlocked at night, as in the case of fire, illness etc. But in the East, at least in Constantinople, locking it should not be neglected.'

A book called *Travelling and Its Requirements, by a Lady*, published by Thomas Cook in 1878, went further: 'Before retiring to rest it is advisable to make a tour of inspection of one's sleeping apartment. In many cases, doors will be found papered over to match the walls and so escape observation; see that these and all others are properly fastened. Do not leave money or valuables in likely places.'

Continuing his advice on staying in a Turkish hotel, Bradshaw said:

'Always have your bill brought the night before leaving and go through it. It is astonishing how many mistakes are made to the detriment of the Tourist; but one never heard of the landlord suffering any loss.

'Soap will never be found; it is always charged extra. Beds should always be well-aired at the fire before sleeping in them, for two excellent reasons, first, they may be damp, most injurious in warm climates, and secondly, the fire is sure to draw out any germs of disease, which may have been left by the last visitor, for few landlords will have their sheets washed after only one night's use. They are merely damped and placed into a press, the same as the table napkins.'

Bradshaw urged his readers to take goods with which to mollify the native population:

'The manners of all are rough, and peculiarly so is their speech; so when some fierce-looking, moustached native addresses you in what appears to be a torrent of abuse, with corresponding gestures, you may be sure that he is only asking trivial questions.

'In curiosity, they beat the Yankees hollow, and you must be prepared to submit to all kinds of questions – what you are, where you are going – *Nereden guerlirsinitz?* – and whether you are not a 'hakim' or doctor.

'This last, every Frank is supposed to be; so a goodly stock

of Morrison's pills will do you good service; and a small magneto-electric machine, some magnesium wire and potassium, will win you such veneration and titles you never dreamt of in your native land. Potassium, which must be kept in naptha, and burns brightly when cast upon water, will astonish them into fits.'

Of the western resident community he was hardly more complimentary: 'There is no society. The various nationalities keep together on a very fair footing, except the English, who are always at loggerheads with one another, or split up into congregations – Presbyterian, Baptist or into anything that will produce dissension.'

A Victorian clergyman, the Rev. J.T.Parfit, one-time Anglican canon of Jerusalem, made a modest fortune from a lantern-slide lecture tour about the Near East. In the course of it, he used to claim, one suspects with a less than Christian regard for truth:

'I was once in an hotel in Constantinople when three residents of the city were watching an American visitor who was obviously very wealthy. One of the three watchers was a Turkish official, another was a Greek money-changer and the third was an Armenian merchant.

'The Turk, with his thumb towards the American, whispered: "I will have his purse."

'The Greek replied with his hand to his mouth: "I have his purse."

The luxury of a Wagon-Lits train sometimes surpassed all but a few grand hotels. Here waiters in eighteenth-century uniforms serve travellers in a Compagnie International dining car.

'The Armenian chuckled and whispered to the Greek: "You had his purse."

'These are then the people who inhabit the Levant, and we call them Levantines. Prejudiced people in the west believe there is a vast deal of difference between the nationalities of the eastern Mediterranean, but they are mistaken.'

The reputation of Constantinople as a town of open sewers, fearsome natives, beggars, thieves and cheating hoteliers spread alongside the fame of the Orient Express. Indeed in one respect the train made it a worse place than it was before: an increase in the numbers of tourists led to a great increase in the numbers and persistence of tourist touts. Eventually it reached the stage at which a visitor being pestered by one cluster of drago-men, as they were called, would be pressed by another group to buy a stick with which to set about the first.

If Nagelmackers could do nothing to induce Constantinople to conform to his customers' expectations of it, he did provide a refuge, a kind of ghetto for wealthy foreigners, to protect them from their local surroundings. It may seem a bizarre sequence of events – to create a train service to a city people would not have visited otherwise, and one they found thoroughly un-congenial, and then create a hotel to give them asylum while they were there; but a large part of the history of tourism has adhered to exactly that pattern, which Nagelmackers pioneered. And there can be no disputing the fact that he pursued it with a sense of magnificence.

In fact he built two hotels, and they were among the very best that the world had ever known. The first of these vast and opulent tourist compounds he built in the diplomatic quarter of Pera, calling it the Pera Palace. Although it is now under different ownership, the Pera Palace flourishes to this day, and it is a worthy if somewhat faded monument to Nagelmackers's grandeur. The public rooms are marble walled, the staircase is mirrored, the glass lift is encased in a shaft of ornate wrought-ironwork. The bedrooms overlooking the Golden Horn are perhaps three times the size of those in modern hotels, and even the private bathrooms are larger than them. Even the mahogany bedsteads imported from Maples of London are still in place.

By the end of 1894 Nagelmackers was advertising the Pera Palace as

'. . . far and away the best hotel . . . situated on the slope of Galata, overlooking the Golden Horn and the whole panorama of Stamboul.

'The Hotel, belonging as it does to the International Sleeping Car Company [the name La Compagnie Internationale called itself in English] is a really modern hotel de luxe, and the only one in the city. It occupies a thoroughly healthy situation, being high up and isolated on all four sides. . . .

OPPOSITE Despite its sordid reputation, Constantinople's exotic magic continued to lure visitors in their thousands: a 1929 poster.

سمبلون
الشرق
اكسبريس
SIMPLON
ORIENT
EXPRESS
COMPAGNIE INTERNATIONALE DES WAGONS-LITS ET DES GRANDS EXPRESS EUROPÉENS
TAU US

Even when tourists ventured outside the hotel, Nagelmackers's men were to hand to ensure that they remained protected: 'The visitor will find every assistance for the proper inspection of the city. Capable dragomen are supplied by the Hotel, who will render every assistance to the uninitiated.'

A few months later Nagelmackers opened his second *hôtel splendide*, the Therapia Summer Palace, across the Straits from Stamboul, 'situated on the shores of the Bosphorus and embedded in the midst of lovely gardens, a veritable terrestrial paradise':

'From the terrace, shaded by venerable vines and cooled by the breezes of the Black Sea, one may view the gay craft and gilded caiques as they glide over the azure surface of the Bosphorus.

'In a word, those who may be seeking a new holiday ground here have their opportunity, for the enterprise of the Company, with its Orient Express and its hotels has, as it were, brought Constantinople to our very doors, so that a holiday in the city of the Sultan is no more difficult of accomplishing from London than one in Paris.'

Nagelmackers's two extraordinary edifices soon became tourist attractions in their own right. The staff conducted themselves with an un-Turkish servility. The menus betrayed no local influence. And so grand were they that some saw little point in venturing outside them to visit the comparatively lacklustre royal palaces.

Despite the apparent inconsistencies, Nagelmackers's eastern venture flourished, except for an interruption for the First World War, right up to 1939; and despite what Constantinople was really like, it occupied for almost half a century a prominent position on the tourist map.

The taming of Constantinople to make it fit for foreign tourists was but the first of many such ventures promoted by Nagelmackers. As new *trains de luxe* came into being, serving an area from Lisbon and Madrid in the south to St Petersburg in the north, so new *hôtels de luxe* sprung up at their destinations. To describe them as palatial was literally accurate: when possible, he bought royal palaces and converted them.

Among the finest examples of Nagelmackers's hotels to survive without compromising their magnificence with modernity are the Avenida Palace in Lisbon and the white-marbled Palace of Madrid, standing across the square from its upstart rival, the Ritz, and with a vast central rotunda for taking afternoon promenades when the weather was too hot to do so outside.

By way of Nagelmackers's Peninsular Express to Brindisi, and thence by fast P & O steamship, Egypt became but six days' journey from London. Soon trains of La Compagnie Internationale were running from Alexandria to Cairo, and from

Cairo to Luxor in the Valley of the Kings, the Star of Egypt Express raced down the banks of the Nile, carrying Edwardian Britain's *literati* to their winter retreat amid the temples. There they spent from November to February in Nagelmackers's Winter Palace Hotel, sketching, writing sonnets to one another and deploring the intrusive arrival of Thomas Cook's hordes on board the sightseeing boats.

In Cairo itself, Nagelmackers bought the Gezireh Palace, an extraordinary folly the Khediv Ismail had built to accommodate the Empress Eugénie, the Prince of Wales, the Russian grand dukes and other members of foreign royalty who had attended the opening ceremonies of the Suez Canal. Each guest found on his arrival that accommodation had been prepared for him that was an exact replica of his private suite in his palace at home.

As Nagelmackers said:

'These were palmy days of uncontrolled expenditure, now followed by practical common sense and a limited liability company.

The Gezireh Palace Hotel, Cairo, in 1897: Nagelmackers's extraordinary folly which, in his own words, was 'the one hotel which absolutely deserves the epithet palatial'. It was converted from a palace by Ismail Pasha.

'The Palace's design [he declared] will still further assist towards the winter depopulation of Europe. Energy, enterprise and genuine art have grappled with the Palace and, so to speak, coaxed it into a hotel. . . .

'One passes through seemingly endless corridors with bachelors' apartments, bathrooms, sitting room, a barber's and a hairdresser's on either side. We pass through the billiards rooms and the splendid bar is reached, but if it is desired to inspect the whole of the hotel in two hours, one must not pause long over this "refresher".

'Ismail's harem, a little north of the main building, will accommodate today two hundred people. . . . A wall fifty yards long brings us to the Arab Kiosque or Casino with its permanent orchestra, a mauresque palace long and low, but beautifully decorated outside and in. . . . To our right across the park are the hotel stables, housing in the season 50 horses, 50 donkeys and some 60 carriages, from broughams to ralli cars. . . .

The Gezireh Palace has not its equal in the world; it is actually, without fiction, the one hotel which absolutely deserves the epithet palatial.'

The feelings of those who regarded themselves as true travellers and who felt an exclusive claim to 'abroad' for themselves and their like were scathing towards the new arrivals. In Cairo, as well as buying the Gezireh Palace and opening it as a hotel, calling in Maples merely to rearrange the furnishings to their best advantage, Nagelmackers acquired control of and refurbished famous Shepheard's; and the following blistering account is one view of the clientele Nagelmackers was bringing to such places as Egypt:

'Inside Shepheards, you will find all the people who live in

The steps in front of the Shepheard's Hotel, Cairo, which Nagelmackers acquired and refurbished and where 'every variation of touts and beggars ogling their prey' were to be seen.

OPPOSITE The smoking pavilion. Patrons of the hotel, according to one account, were people who have 'been everywhere and done nothing . . . people who spoil the globe by travelling on it'.

their boxes and grand hotels, who know all lands but no languages, who have been everywhere and done nothing, looked at everything and seen nothing, read everything and know nothing – who spoil the globe by travelling on it.

'And outside is the native complement of them – guides and donkey boys, hawkers of matches and piastre toys, rigged up in Bedouin garb as bogus as the wares they purvey or – on commission – persuade tourists to buy, every variation of touts and beggars waylaying their prey.'

The author of the above remarks, a now-forgotten travel writer, may not be regarded as the most objective of observers – remarking that on his first trip down the Nile Thomas Cook's son and heir, John Mason Cook, threw an argumentative dragoman into the river 'to think matters over'. He stated: 'A man like this was just the man for Egypt.'

The resentment towards the new tourists of those who had travelled before the days of Nagelmackers's *trains de luxe* and grand hotels was vented in the letters column of *The Times*, where angry writers expostulated over their arrogance, ignorance, bad manners and offensive conduct. Adam Smith

remarked that they 'commonly return home more conceited, more unprincipled and more dissipated'. In France the arrival of large numbers of unpleasant English holidaymakers gave rise to the publication of a new weekly journal, *L'Anti-Anglais*, whose slogan was 'SUS AUX ANGLAIS!' and which asked in every issue, without fail: '*Qui a brûlé Jeanne d'Arc?* Remember!'

Accounts were published of the grossness of the English traveller abroad. One described how a '*milord*', visiting Lausanne with his lady, commissioned a firework display. When he arrived at the valley where it was to be held he was infuriated to see that a crowd of Swiss had turned up to watch the show as well and promptly cancelled it on the grounds that he had intended it for the enjoyment of himself and his wife alone. That night there was a storm, a bolt of lightning set the display alight and *milord* was incensed when he was denied a refund.

'It is astonishing [wrote a correspondent to the *Traveller's Journal*] how the English may always be distinguished by their invariably choosing to do everything in a manner and at a time when no-one else would.

'One in particular amused me when he took his place at dinner in a French hotel, leaving space for half a dozen or more between the other guests and himself.

'He consoled himself the first day, in his insulated greatness, by calling for wines which the house did not afford; and when they were at length procured for him, he found them so novel to his palate and uncongenial to his stomach, that he was obliged to have recourse to the vulgarity of qualifying them with cognac. . . .

'After dinner, he remained alone with his dessert and wine at a small table but alas! the newspaper, that silent, best companion of an Englishman's self-concentrated sociability, was wanting; and to supply its place, he gravely took out his passport and, with an abstracted, businesslike air, held it at arm's length from his eyes and, with both legs on the chair opposite him, read it through, probably for the hundredth time, from beginning to end.'

Despite such mockery and abuse, the British remained La Compagnie Internationale's best customers (the Germans coming second in number), to the extent that it eventually bought controlling interests in Thomas Cook and Dean & Dawson to protect the market from competition. In due course, in succession to Nagelmackers, his English son-in-law, Lord Dalziel, took charge of La Compagnie Internationale itself.

By the closing years of the nineteenth century British railway companies had become alarmed at the numbers of rich travellers going abroad for their holidays instead of remaining in England, and launched what was intended to be a surreptitious campaign to denigrate 'abroad' and sing the praises of the English country-

LEFT Visitors enjoy a 'picnic' in the Mustra Valley, Egypt, 1899.

BELOW A rest for tourists and their guides at the foot of the pyramids.

LE MONDE
OÙ
L'ON S'AMUSE

The Continental Express was one of several magazines launched to encourage more Britons to leave their native shores: an extract from a 1909 issue.

Biarritz.

Failure of Women's Sweepstake. THE weather has not been exceptionally nice this Christmas at Biarritz, and Golfers have been obliged to play under somewhat depressing conditions. Princess Fredrika of Hanover has been seen a great deal on the links just recently, and on New Year's Day made a big score against Admiral Johnson. The customary Women's Christmas Sweepstake did not prove a big success, the number required being fifteen, and only an unlucky thirteen were entered. The Competition has, however, been postponed, and will change its name to the New Year Handicap.

Big Children's Party. AT the Casino Bellevue on the 4th great preparations had been made for the Children's fête, and between two and three thousand children were assembled under its holly-bedecked walls. The noise and shrieks of delight can be better imagined than described when the Christmas trees were illuminated and despoiled of their treasures.

London Motor-'Buses for the Pyrenées. A SYNDICATE is being formed to supply the golfers a modern means of conveyance between the town and the links, and the report of the committee sent to decide the best form of car suitable for Biarritz and its environs was discussed. It appears that the travels of these latter took them as far as the English Metropolis, and they have decided the English style of motor-'bus as being far superior to those of Berlin and Paris. This seems rather strange to us, for we were under the impression that the only portion of the bus manufactured without the foreign label in

Croquet at Biarritz.

— 5 —

side and resorts. A journal entitled *Travel*, which was ostensibly independent editorially and which, at first sight, appeared to be promoting travel abroad, was actually distributed free of charge by railway companies. One not untypical leading article spoke of

'. . . the factors which keep the Englishman so much in his own isles.

'An Englishman, when he passes from the scenes of his own south to the assimilated district in the neighbouring country of France finds a tameness, a want of animation and relief, which tells him at once he is in another and a foreign country.

'He glides down the beautiful Seine to find a country spoiled for want of care, and a district of great capability wearing the face of a comparative desert. None of the bright fields of his native land, no beautiful cattle spreading over the distant scene. . . . It is this which induces, to some extent, the English tourist to pass so much of his time in the native land, added to the fact that the continental system of travelling is so much more irksome than our own.'

An article was reprinted from the *St James's Gazette*, describing the insufferable impertinence of German stationmasters:

'In recent years, he has reached a giddy height of power. A few years ago, he could only prove his high station by bestowing a stony stare on you if you asked for information, without first giving the requisite number of bows, or by falling into an apoplectic fit when a fourth-class passenger sat on a seat while waiting for a train. . . .

'But that was long ago. Not only is no one now allowed on the platform without a ticket, but the unfortunate traveller is not allowed off it unless he is provided with a permit by the Stationmaster.

'So you proceed to pay your humble petition before him. If you approach him in a familiar manner or with insufficient humility, he will utterly ignore you, turning away and proceeding to his office as if he had never seen you, for a Stationmaster on the Prussian State Railways is worth some dozen passengers. But by showing becoming deference, he will graciously condescend to ask you if there is anything he can do for you.

'If you are an experienced traveller, you recognise his all-powerfulness and, making obeisance before him, humbly inform him that he himself sent you there and you want to leave the station. If he is in a good temper, your humility propitiates him, and he may venture a remark about the weather. Thus chatting amiably, he glances through several documents, and signs a report or two before going to a drawer in his desk. Bringing out a small india-rubber stamp, he impresses on the back of your ticket a legend which states that you are permitted to leave the precincts of such and such a station on such and such a date by order of So and so, Stationmaster. Filling in the correct date and signing his name, he then returns your ticket with a bow if he is an affable man; if not with the remark that it is a great nuisance and that passengers ought to take a ticket to the station at which they want to alight.'

Foreigners in your compartment could also be a blight. One report told of an English gentleman who mounted a second-class carriage in Prussia and attempted to engage the two ladies there in amicable conversation. After a while, one of them broke their stony silence with the remark: 'Sir, it would seem that you have never travelled second class before, and do not know how to behave.'

'I must confess, madame, I have not,' replied the Englishman, for once getting the upper hand. 'I have previously travelled

THEIR MAJESTIES'
SILVERSMITH, JEWELLER,
AND
DRESSING CASE
MANUFACTURER.

J. C. VICKERY.

179, 181, 183,
REGENT ST.,
LONDON, W.

No. P 1953.

Vickery's Most Successful Registered
Best Silk Covered Eiderdown Travelling
Rug with attached Foot Muff.

It also has Muff for the Hands
and Useful Pockets for Hand-
kerchief, Purse, etc., and Down
Cushion to match, complete in
Limp Leather Case to match,
with Handle for carrying.

	4 by 4ft. Rug.	5½ by 4ft. Rug.
Moss Green, Dark Blue, Violet or Brown	£7 5 0	£7 18 6
Dark Brown Pigskin	8 8 0	9 9 0

TRAVELLING RUG,
CUSHION, AND FOOT MUFF
IN COMPACT CASE.
VERY LIGHT AND PORTABLE.

Very suitable for ——
Motoring, Driving, or for long Railway Journeys, etc., etc.

Travel accessory
advertisement, 1909.

only by first and third class. I have observed that in first class,
the passengers insult the railway staff, whereas in the third class
the railway staff insult the passengers. Now I learn that in
second class, the passengers insult each other.'

Another Englishman travelling on the continent, Lord
Russell, was acclaimed for putting a native with whom he was
sharing a compartment in his place. As the train drew out of the
station the foreigner proceeded to open his carpet-bag, take out
a pair of slippers and untie the laces of his shoes.

'If you do that, sir,' proclaimed the great Victorian jurist,
'I shall throw your shoes out of the window.'

The foreigner remarked that he had a right to do as he wished
in his own country, so long as he did not inconvenience others.
Lord Russell demurred. The man took off his shoes, and Lord
Russell threw them out of the window.

Yet another article told of the phoney Belgian baggage
inspector who allegedly haunted Nagelmackers's trains depart-
ing from Ostend. Equipped with a cheap season ticket and a
steel measure one metre long he would enter a compartment,
engage the passengers in cordial conversation and then whip
out his rule, measure a suitcase, 'assume his official bearing and
address the owner with becoming severity as follows: "Sir,
your portmanteau is five centimetres over the prescribed length.
I am one of the company's inspectors and charge you at once
five francs tax on unauthorised luggage."' And the timorous
English paid up to the scoundrel.

For several centuries it had been, as it still is, an axiom of the
English that the French were far less polite than they used to be;
and not even this chestnut was left unroasted by the anti-abroad
propagandists. 'Everyone must admit that a certain change has
come over the manners of the French nation,' *Travel* averred,

OPPOSITE Cigarette
cards depicting
locomotives from around
the world.

OVERLEAF The opening
of the Yokohama-
Tokyo Railway, which
provided another
overland link for
around-the-world
tourists.

WILL'S CIGARETTES.

EGYPTIAN STATE RAILWAYS.

WILLS'S CIGARETTES.

SOUTH AFRICAN RAILWAYS.

WILLS'S CIGARETTES.

ITALIAN STATE RAILWAYS.

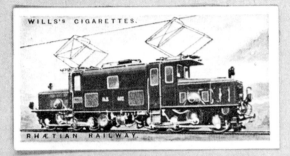

WILLS'S CIGARETTES.

RHÆTIAN RAILWAY.

WILLS'S CIGARETTES.

WESTERN RAILWAY OF FRANCE.

WILLS'S CIGARETTES.

PALESTINE RAILWAYS.

WILLS'S CIGARETTES.

BELGIAN STATE RAILWAYS.

WILLS'S CIGARETTES.

NORTHERN RAILWAY OF SPAIN.

THE CAPITOL LIMITED
BALTIMORE & OHIO RAILROAD.

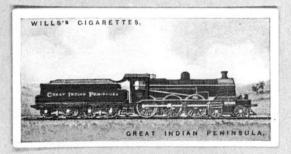

WILLS'S CIGARETTES.

GREAT INDIAN PENINSULA.

汐留より蒸気車通行の圖

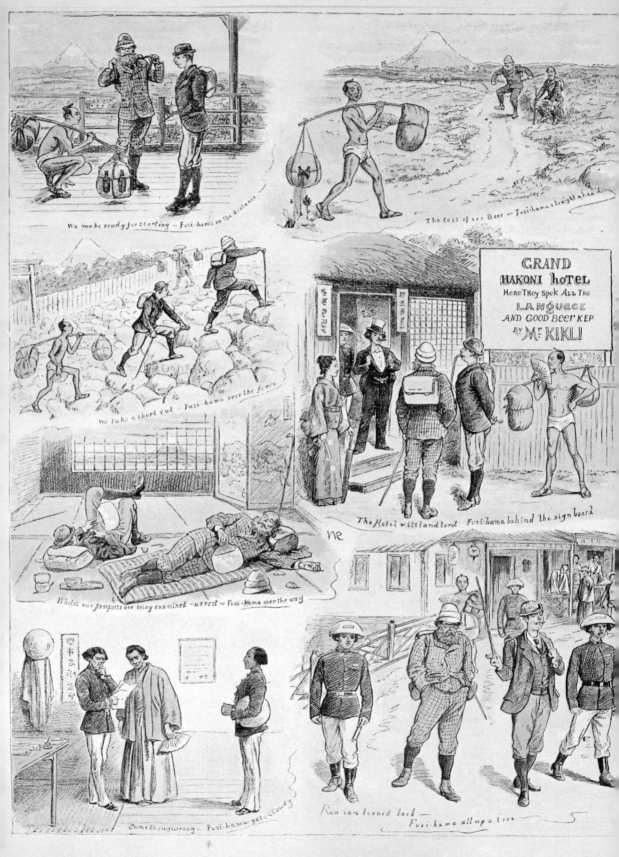

TOURISTS IN JAPAN—TRYING TO CLIMB FUSI-HAMA

citing 'an anecdote from the Palais Royal to illustrate rather forcibly the new idea of good manners':

'A gentleman takes a vacant place in a restaurant very near to another without addressing a word to him.

'The two sit silent until the newcomer, in manipulating his iced seltzer, spurts a drop by accident over the cutlet of his neighbour. He omits to apologise, and the latter instantly calls the waiter and orders a fresh cutlet.

'This is too much at last for the equanimity of the intruder, who takes out his purse and for the first time addressing the other, says: "I shall pay for your cutlet, sir."

The ice might seem to be broken, and a reconciliation half affected. But the offended is still equal to the occasion. "I should hope you would, sir," he laconically replies, and lapses into silence.'

Quelle horreur!

The dangers of contracting cholera and other fatal diseases on the continent were lingeringly and highly exaggeratedly explored. The unsuitability of meats cooked in garlic and oil – it seemed that the Europeans knew no other way in the kitchen – was dealt with at length. The pervasiveness of Jews in foreign resorts and spas was duly noted, and the grasping nature of hoteliers, the poor quality of the cigars and above all the treacherous lengths to which foreigners who pretended to befriend and help British visitors would go in pretending were all covered in their turn.

An illustration of the latter was provided by an English gentleman who, to oblige a foreign lady whom he had met abroad, volunteered to take for her a parcel to her son, then living in London. She entrusted to him a tin labelled 'processed peas' with a great show of gratitude. It was only on delivering it that he discovered, to his shock and amazement, that it contained not peas but tobacco, on which excise duty should have been paid. 'No doubt', commented 'A Correspondent' of *Travel*, 'the young gentleman's mama chuckled at her own ingenuity when she confided her "tin of peas" to the trunk of an unsuspecting English traveller.'

But the British promoters of the anti-abroad travel movement delighted most particularly in 'outrages' perpetrated against the English on the continent. These tended to be given little or no attention in the daily press, presumably because the editors concerned, in their wisdom, suspected that they had been provoked by the offensive behaviour of the English concerned. Thus *Travel*, upbraiding the newspapers for ignoring the affair, described the 'outrage' perpetrated – as a result of what provocation it omitted to mention – against a Major Harding, his daughter, Mr Glover of the War Office, Mr Wragg, a solicitor, and Mr Wimble, an architect, who went on holiday to Hamburg together.

OPPOSITE Inscrutable Western tourists in the course of trying to climb a mountain during a railway adventure in Japan.

COOK—WAGONS-LITS INTERPRETERS

The Continental Express.

Riviera Sketches.

trains and hotels and doing away with the necessity for being at a railway station an hour before the train starts.

These waits, however, are not always tedious, and at Marseilles in particular, the cosmopolitan crowd is a source of ever-changing interest.

Next door to the Riviera and on the great highway 'twixt east and west, its railway station is thronged not only by travellers from far afield, but by all the latest vagaries of fashion, worn by those who from all parts of Europe are on their way to see and be seen under the bright, staring sun of the south.

Trucks filled with baggage that proclaim its nationality are continually, and often forcibly, crossing the path of the anxious traveller. What a medley of size and shape, of youth and age. Old trunks, new trunks, leather trunks and trunks of cane, the well cared for and the shabby and neglected.

Curious packages, both large and small, that have rubbed shoulders with many a porter and novice, plastered over with endless hotel labels until they look like movable advertisement hoardings deceiving to the uninitiated, for doubtless in this up-to-date age there must be agencies who can supply any number of hotel labels to the untravelled at a nominal cost. I never can understand any self-respecting man allowing his baggage to be plastered over with gaudy pictures of indifferent hotels, works of art that would in most cases be unworthy of an Italian ice-cream barrow.

And how these bags of all sizes and weights are bundled into carriages that obviously were not intended for such heavy 'loads'! Racks are strained and timid travellers kept in constant anxiety lest a sudden jerk should bring an avalanche as

ABOVE LEFT Uniformed interpreters were on duty at all international railway stations to assist a new generation of monoglot travellers.

RIGHT Illustration from *The Continental Express*, 1909.

One morning they left on a day's visit to Frankfurt-am-Main. As they lunched there at the Café Casino, opposite the Frankfurterhof, 'a waiter informed Mr Wimble that two gentlemen were desirous of speaking to him'. On going to the entrance, 'he was pounced upon by two German detectives as one of several persons they were seeking.' The whole group was rounded up and 'peremptorily directed' to the police station, where they were 'placed in a room under the guardianship of two police officers, and warned not to speak to each other'. Major Harding now took up the tale:

'I was summoned to the presence of the two detectives, together with a third person evidently inferior to them. I was asked for my name, address, my age, the date and place of my birth, my address here and in England.

'These I wrote down. I produced my pocket book, which was snatched from my hand and thrown upon a table. My vest was roughly opened by them, my watch, locket and chain taken from me and *my trouser buttons examined*.

'I protested against their conduct, and demanded to see the British Consul. This was refused.

'A man was called in to take me away. I requested to see my daughter before going. This was brutally refused. I was taken to a cell and locked in.'

By late that evening the British vice-consul, Herr Goldbeck, had heard by chance of what had happened, and intervened to effect their release and to put them up in his own home for the night.

But the outrage was not yet over. Returning to Hamburg the next day, they went to their hotel to find that the police had called in their absence and searched their portmanteaus. As Mr Wragg the solicitor commented in a letter to *Travel*:

'. . . to make the treatment I experienced the more unpardonable, I am

A Member of Stephen's Club

and

Of the City Carlton Club.'

'Certainly,' stormed *Travel*, 'Lord Salisbury is not the man to let an affair of this kind "slide".' For whatever reason, Lord Salisbury and the Foreign Office did, despite the increasingly strident demands for action in successive issues of the journal.

Hardly had the editors recovered their composure following the Frankfurt Outrage, than another came to their notice, in Geneva. Their account was attributed to 'One Who Knows the Facts'. It described how the Swiss police followed a Mr Lowndes from the railway station to his rooms, and kept a watch on the premises for several hours. Then they entered by force, roused him from his bed and ransacked his daughter's wardrobe 'in a very offensive manner'. But that was nothing compared with the offensiveness that was to follow.

Mr Lowndes, needless to say, spoke not a word of any language but English; but his daughter knew some French and asked them what they were doing. They explained that they were searching for an international thief, and showed her a photograph they had. She assured the police that the picture bore no resemblance to her father.

'Perhaps not to your father, miss,' was the damnably insolent reply, 'but to this gentleman here.'

Again the British consulate was alerted and came to the rescue. But as One Who Knows the Facts pertinently remarked:

'When a well-known and highly respected family is annoyed in this manner, no one feels safe.

'Unless these dunderheaded detectives get something more than a rap over the knuckles for their obtuseness, *the Continent will be shunned by British tourists as they would shun a plague spot*.'

To counter the propaganda barrage against abroad, in 1894 Nagelmackers launched his own journal in Britain, *The Continental Traveller*, distributing copies of it to Buckingham and St James's Palaces, Marlborough House, Mansion House, the Guildhall, the Houses of Parliament, the Stock Exchange and the principal clubs for gentlemen.

The Continental Traveller detailed the comforts and pleasures provided by La Compagnie Internationale's *trains de luxe*, with lavish illustrations and detailed plans of their amenities:

ABOVE, RIGHT and OPPOSITE Illustrations from *The Traveller* (1909) showing the 'elegant and comfortable' amenities offered on the *train de luxe*.

'The appointments of the Sleeping Carriages are elegant and comfortable in every respect.

'The beds are as comfortable as those found in any high class hotel, special attention being directed to the proper airing of all bed linen, which is of the best quality and always kept scrupulously clean. . . . The car attendants in almost every instance speak English and generally two or three other languages. . . . Each car has a servant, whose duty it is to brush the clothes, varnish the boots, make the beds and generally attend on the passengers.

'The restaurant car tariff is very moderate: the morning café au lait, 1s.; luncheon, 3s. 3d.; dinner 4s. 10d. Wines and liqueurs are carried in great variety – they are to be found of good quality and at reasonable prices.

'Nothing, in fact, has been neglected which can give the passenger the illusion that he is in a good hotel.'

Introducing the new Ostend–Vienna Express to English travellers, the journal claimed that it

'. . . appears to have been adopted by the German and Austrian courts as their special means of intercommunication between Cologne, Frankfort, Vienna and London, as witness the recent journey to London and return of the Archduke Ferdinand of Austria, and others. There is no surer guarantee of the comfort of a train than the presence of Royalty as ordinary passengers.

There are no surer judges either of the speed and general use-fulness of a train than the Queen's Messengers, who have already adopted it as the proper and quickest means of getting to all the capitals of that part of Europe which are served by this train.'

Nagelmackers need not have troubled himself. The energy with which the English railway companies pursued their campaign of denigration of foreigners and foreign countries was evidence enough of his success in luring the English abroad.

The Blue Train, or Train Bleu, leaving Paris with its cargo of aristocrats, gamblers, social climbers and disinherited Russian princes.

7. Le Train Bleu

'Le Train Bleu', as Nagelmackers's Calais–Paris–Nice Express came to be known, thanks to its blue and gold livery, with its mixed cargo of English aristocrats, merchants' wives with marriageable daughters, well-heeled gamblers, American social climbers and Russian princes, steamed to the French Riviera for the first time in December 1883.

Launched by Nagelmackers but three months after the Orient Express, the Train Bleu was still more luxurious. It contained the first travelling cocktail bar and a 'Pergola Restaurant'; even the corridors were carpeted in deep pile and the accommodation was so spacious, as well as being ornate, that only ten people were carried in each coach, under the charge of a servant-valet of La Compagnie Internationale.

If the aura of the Orient Express was one of mystique, excitement and fleeting, illicit romance, that of the Train Bleu was straightforwardly one of glamour. The former was commemorated in romantic novelettes, thrillers and a Parisian music hall show. The latter was honoured by a ballet by Diaghilev.

Together with its complementing palace hotels at Cimiez, above Nice, and La Turbie, looking down on the principality of Monaco, the Train Bleu played an important role in transforming that stretch of Provençal coastline into the Côte d'Azur, the world's most fabled pleasure resort. Here Queen Victoria and her court, and much of the Russian and German ones, were to reassemble; new fashions for the whole of Europe were to be seen each season; each winter girls unwillingly betrothed to barons were to elope with hotel violinists; the bodies of young noblemen were to be found, bullets through the roofs of their mouths, in the casino gardens; and the Fitzgeralds were to cut their swathe through society, here Scott pelting the Princess de Carmen-Chimay with figs to enliven a formal dinner, there Zelda flinging herself head-first down a flight of stone steps to divert her husband from his attentions to Isadora Duncan.

For the upper classes of Europe and especially of Britain, the inauguration of the Train Bleu marked the beginning of a new kind of social season, and a new style of travel. The novelty was considerable. Previously one had gone abroad for a purpose – to view ancient monuments and galleries of pictures, or for the sake of one's health. The purpose of the annual winter retreat to the south of France was pleasure.

The British began the journey at Victoria Station. Trunks filled with the new season's fashions from Bond Street were unloaded from the hansom and entrusted to a porter, not to be seen again until arrival in Nice. Then across the station yard to Overton's Restaurant for a luncheon of a dozen or two Whitstable oysters, grilled sole, Stilton cheese and a bottle of Chablis, served by avuncular English waiters in long white aprons. Then

one returned to the station platform where the Club Train awaited, the precursor of the Golden Arrow and Nagelmackers's only incursion into England. At the entrance to each carriage stood its conductor, dressed in the chocolate brown livery of La Compagnie Internationale. He took one to one's reserved coupé, relieved one of one's passport and tickets so that one need not be disturbed during the journey, and offered champagne or other refreshments.

The train passed through the green Kent countryside to Dover, where a steam packet of the London, Chatham and Dover Railway Company, for the exclusive use of Club Train passengers, was at the quayside. It took three hours to cross to Calais, where the Train Bleu itself awaited.

Installed in a still more luxurious private compartment, one was rushed to Paris where, as the train passed around the

A diorama spectacular showing the fashionable and famous gathering for the departure of the Train Bleu.

OPPOSITE The train's minute kitchen, where the chef triumphed above adverse conditions to produce elaborate meals of five courses.

Le Train Bleu

ceinture to meet up with other carriages from Berlin, St Petersburg, Warsaw, Vienna and elsewhere, one spent a two hour excursion, perhaps doing some last-minute shopping in the Rue de Rivoli.

Boarding the now fully-sized Train Bleu, it was time to change for dinner and to go to the Pergola Restaurant to consume soup, fish, meat, cheese and dessert and, more attentively, to survey the other passengers for familiar faces and new fashions.

The train reached the Mediterranean coast at Marseilles the next day. The passengers gazed upon Cassis and the beautiful azure sea with the occasional fishing boat. The train wound its way along the coast and through tunnels to Antibes and the Baie des Anges and thence to Nice.

A common means of installing yourself for the season was to deposit your baggage, repair to the Hôtel des Anglais, order lunch and instruct the concierge to contact some estate agents to attend upon you. These latter would arrive with deferential haste to show you particulars of the villas and apartments available for rent through the season, and you composed a short list of those to be inspected while you ate. By teatime, you would be installed, and by the end of the next day, you had

The Promenade des Anglais in Nice, one of the most famous walks in the world, which was constructed by the English community to ameliorate local unemployment. After the inauguration of the Train Bleu it became the focal point of the Riviera's winter season.

signed the visitors' book at the British Consulate, arranged for your arrival to be noted in the local press, and made a first round of calls with visiting cards.

From as early as October to the following February, life would be a round of *thé-dansants* and charity balls, dinner parties and promenades, shopping in the local branches of Parisian stores, sketching the scenery, having dresses made and the like.

Nice had been the winter refuge of some of the English aristocracy and men of letters for a century before Italy ceded it, virtually at gunpoint, to France in 1861. As early as 1763, the English novelist Dr Tobias Smollett settled there, renting a flat on the ground floor with a garden for £20 per annum, and writing tracts on the great benefits that accrued to the health by bathing in the sea there. Smollett's pamphleteering, the prescriptions by fashionable London physicians of a few months in the south of France as a cure for almost any ailment from tuberculosis to *ennui* and the gradual emergence in Nice of something resembling what the English upper classes were pleased to call society, combined to make the town, from October to March, an English colony in almost all but name.

Soon after the beginning of the nineteenth century Nice acquired its first modern hotel, the German-owned Hôtel des Anglais. By 1882 the English winter community was sufficiently numerous, established and rich to mitigate greatly the otherwise disastrous effect of a freak frost that destroyed the orange crop, and at the same time to facilitate its own access to the beach by commissioning the local peasantry to construct the Promenade des Anglais. And shortly after Nice became part of France, it was linked by railway with Paris and Calais. Hotels sprang up along the promenade. English people formed their own *quartier* at Cimiez, building lavish private villas there. From October onwards, they left their visiting cards in one another's homes, entertained one another to tea and musical soirées, founded an Anglican church and formed a Society for the Prevention of Cruelty to Animals.

The arrival of *trains de luxe* in the Riviera from all the major capitals of Europe transformed the area in a few years into a rip-roaring pleasure resort; and a bitter fight broke out over the spoils the trains brought with them.

The extraordinary battle which Nice and Monte Carlo waged between each other for the custom of Nagelmackers's passengers has been obscured by the passing of time and the smoothing-over of unpleasantness by tourist authorities. I have reconstructed it as best I can from often conflicting contemporary press accounts because it is evidence as striking as it is little known of the impact that the introduction of international train services could have on a previously peaceful and somewhat obscure corner of Europe.

127

NICE (CIMIEZ).

The Riviera Palace

Furnished throughout by Maple & Co., of Tottenham Court Road,
London, and Rue Boudreau, Paris.

INT. WAGONS-LITS CO.
SUMMER
ON THE FRENCH RIVIERA
BY THE
BLUE TRAIN

ABOVE The Riviera Palace, an exclusive hotel in the English quarter of Nice. It was one of the first of an international chain of 'Palace' hotels, stretching from Lisbon to Peking, built by Nagelmackers.

ABOVE RIGHT An advertising brochure from the twenties for the Train Bleu. Having established the Riviera as a winter resort of the aristocracy, La Compagnie Internationale promoted it as a summer playground for the middle classes.

While the population of Nice increased tenfold in a decade to serve the influx of semi-resident foreigners, Monaco, a few miles along the coast, was faced with the prospect of bankruptcy. Originally the principality extended far beyond its present tiny frontiers, to the Italian border. It lived less than modestly from the export of olive oil, oranges and lemons. As the fiefdom's only source of national revenue was a tax on such exports, and as that tax served more to price its produce out of the French market – the only one available to it – than to line the pseudo-royal coffers, drastic action was required if it was not to fall like a rotting orange into the hands of the French government through insolvency.

The nature of the drastic action Prince Charles espied through the success of the Grand Duke of Baden. The Grand Duke had made his town the leading spa of Europe by the expedient of providing (in addition to the normal medical facilities) a casino where one might gamble legally and in public. Almost throughout Europe gaming establishments were regarded by respectable society as more or less akin to brothels. Like brothels, they were outlawed on the statute book but flourished in private. European society was suitably outraged by the Grand Duke's move in not merely legalizing gambling, but placing the casino at Baden-Baden under state ownership and control. Baden-Baden duly became the most frequented summer resort; and to avoid extinction the rival spas had to follow suit.

Prince Charles had no money for launching such an attraction to draw gamblers to the principality during the winter. He raised it by selling, in the same year as the annexation of Nice, all those parts of Monaco that Napoleon III was willing to buy on France's behalf. These included Menton, later to prosper from its reputation as a last resting place for the widows of empire builders and colonial bishops, and Roquebrune, the retreat in this century of Sir Winston Churchill, Greek shipping millionaires and their respective and intermingling circles. After the deal was done Charles and the handful of subjects that remained to him were left with eight square miles of rocky fields, where a few straggling olive and citrus trees somehow contrived to survive. The French government, having reduced Monaco to a pimple on its behind, waited impatiently for the whole absurd structure of an unviable state to collapse.

Instead Charles used the money Napoleon had paid him to build a gambling casino and two hotels. The rest of Europe was predictably outraged in its censures, and failed to arrive. The reason was that Monaco was unappealing and inaccessible.

Facing bankruptcy once more, Charles saved his own puny throne and the principality itself by selling out again. M. François Blanc, who had begun life as a waiter, gone as such to Baden-Baden, moved from restaurant to casino and from Baden-Baden to Bad Homburg to establish one there for a percentage of the profits, bought an exclusive concession from Charles to run gambling in Monaco; and he did not repeat Charles's mistake of scrimping on the surroundings in which clients were to be relieved of their money.

It was Blanc who coined the axiom: 'Money paid to a gambler is not lost, only lent.' His casino, still the world's finest, reflected his confidence in the future of his trade both in its opulence and in its extent. By dint of its sheer magnificence, its renown began to spread. Within a year of the railway's reaching Monaco, in 1868, Prince Charles, although the recipient of a minute royalty on the takings of M. Blanc's Casino Royal, was able to abolish all forms of taxation and begin to build himself a fine palace. (M. Blanc himself cannot be said to have suffered from the deal, leaving an estate—astonishing for the time—of almost £4 million.)

The response of the city fathers of Nice was to seek to portray Monte Carlo to the world as the epitome of sin and dissolution, and their own town as that of respectability and rectitude. It was at that time that the scandal of the Monte Carlo suicides was unleashed on the world.

That some young men went to Monte Carlo to break the bank, only to break themselves instead and to commit suicide in the casino's grounds is perfectly possible, and perhaps even true. But it is also the case that new public venues attract would-be suicides as fly-paper attracts flies. Thus when the first grand hotels opened in the United States early in the nineteenth century, a notably high proportion of those who wished to kill themselves chose to do so not at home, as they would, perforce, have had to do before, but by booking them-

Répartition des décès par Cause et par Mois

NUMÉROS D'ORDRE	CAUSES DE DÉCÈS	Janvier	Février	Mars	Avril	Mai	Juin	Juillet	Août	Septembre	Octobre	Novembre	Décembre	TOTAL
1	Fièvre typhoïde (typhus abdominal)		1		2			1	1	3	2		1	11
2	Typhus exanthématique													
3	Fièvre et cachexie paludéennes													
4	Variole													
5	Rougeole		1											1
6	Scarlatine													
7	Coqueluche													
8	Diphtérie et croup	1												1
9	Grippe	1												1
10	Choléra asiatique													
11	Choléra nostras													
12	Autres maladies épidémiques		1						1					2
13	Tuberculose des poumons	5	8	3	2	1	4	5	3	4	1		3	39
14	Tuberculose des méninges			2	1	1								4
15	Autres tuberculoses			1	1	2	2	1			1			8
16	Cancer et autres tumeurs malignes	4	2	2	1	4	1			2		1	3	20
17	Méningite simple		2	4	1		1							8
18	Hémorragie et ramollissement du cerveau	4	2	2	1		1	3	3	1	4	1		22
19	Maladies organiques du cœur	2	5	2	6	3	3		1	4	2	2	5	35
20	Bronchite aiguë	2	1	1								1		5
21	Bronchite chronique											3	1	4
22	Pneumonie	5	7							1		2	1	16
23	Autres affections de l'appareil respiratoire (phtisie exceptée)	12	5	4	2	2	1	2	1	1	2	2		34
24	Affections de l'estomac (cancer excepté)										1			1
25	Diarrhée et entérite (au-dessous de deux ans)	1				1	1	1	2					6
26	Appendicite et typhite													
27	Hernie, obstruction intestinale													
28	Cirrhose de foie		1	2	2					2			1	8
29	Néphrite aiguë et maladie de Bright	1			1	2							2	6
30	Tumeurs non cancéreuses et autres affections des org. gén. de la femme													
31	Septicémie puerpérale (fièvre, péritonite phlébite puerpérales)	1	2				1				1		1	6
32	Autres accidents puerpéraux de la grossesse et de l'accouchement													
33	Débilité congle et vices de conformation	1				1	1				1	1		5
34	Sénilité			2	1	1		2	3	1	1			11
35	Morts violentes (suicide excepté)	3	2		1	1			2			1	3	13
36	Suicide	1	2	1	2	1		4	1	1				13
37	Autres maladies	4	5	5	6	3	1		1	5	2	3	2	37
38	Maladie inconnue ou mal définie				2									2
39														
40														
	TOTAUX	48	47	31	32	23	17	19	19	25	18	17	23	319

SUICIDES

MENTON

Lundi une dame pénétrait dans une maison de la rue Palmaro, entrait dans une chambre ouverte où dînaient les locataires, et se tirant un coup de revolver dans la bouche, se tuait raide.

Au bruit de la détonation une foule compacte a envahi les escaliers et la chambre où cette malheureuse s'était tuée. Le juge de paix, la gendarmerie et les agents de police sont arrivés et ont fait évacuer l'appartement.

Les constatations légales et médicales ont été faites : la mort a été instantanée.

On a trouvé dans une poche de sa robe, un billet ainsi libellé :

« Si vous voulez en connaître plus long, adres-
» sez-vous à M. Chartran, directeur du Casino de
» Monaco. »

GOLFE-JUAN

Avant-hier, une jeune fille, âgée de 20 ans, Mlle S. M..., s'est donné volontairement la mort en se jetant au fond d'un puits.

On attribue cet acte de désespoir à la rupture de son mariage, dûe aux *pertes énormes* subies à Monte-Carlo par son fiancé.

selves into a room and turning on the gas. In like manner, railways were given a bad name in their early years by the numbers of people who chose to fling themselves under on-rushing engines or from the platforms of expresses passing over viaducts. So it was with new bridges and so it seems to have been with Monte Carlo – it became its fate to be the fashionable place from which to dispatch oneself.

But not even this penchant for leaving the world in style explains the quite extraordinary numbers of bodies that were found, if not every day, then several mornings a week in the gardens of the casino at Monte Carlo in the 1880s. After all no such phenomenon had resulted from the opening of casinos in Baden-Baden, Bad Godesberg, Bad Homburg or other German spas. A reasonable supposition is that the city fathers of Nice were collecting, for a sum, suitable bodies of people who had died in their own locality, firing a revolver into their mouths *post mortem*, and smuggling them into the neighbouring principality during the night. How otherwise would the sound of the gunfire not have been heard over the hush of the nearby gaming tables? More pertinently, how otherwise could the 'suicides' have been ended so abruptly by M. Blanc agreeing to pay Nice a fat sum of money?

Whatever the truth of the matter, the press of Europe, from

Rivalry between Nice and Monte Carlo for the custom of visitors arriving on the Train Bleu was fierce and unscrupulous. ABOVE LEFT Bloodcurdling propaganda issued by the anti-casino lobby describing non-existent suicides allegedly due to losses at roulette.

OPPOSITE Record of deaths in Monaco in 1912. The Monégasque authorities felt obliged to publish them to counter rumours of suicides caused by gambling losses.

ABOVE A decorative railway poster for Monaco, designed by Alphonse Mucha.

Jean Béraud
1890

Le Train Bleu

PREVIOUS PAGES *Rien ne va plus* (no more bets): a portrayal of Fernand Blanc's casino at Monte Carlo in 1890.

Rome and Odessa to Paris and London, raged against the iniquitious occurrences that took place in the principality. Photographs of dubious authenticity, portraying gentlemen in evening clothes lying dead in a pool of blood, a revolver butt still gripped by their right hands, the barrel still in their lips, were widely circulated, together with lurid reports.

The performance of Nice's city fathers would in no way have shamed the news managers of the misinformation departments of the KGB and the CIA today. In the course of a single winter season, they began by inspiring the following report in *The Times* of London:

'THE MONTE CARLO SCANDAL

'Pending the early resumption of the agitation against the Monte Carlo iniquities, several facts may be noted. . . . Owing to the suicide of an American officer, ruined at Monaco, the American naval anchorage and victualling establishments have been given up and sold, Leghorn now being the Mediterranean station. The Russian navy has also deserted Nice, while even the French evolution squadron shuns it, and Admiral Krantz, who till lately commanded it, made no secret of the fact that the rarity of his visits was owing to the existence of Monte Carlo.

'Spontaneous protests against Monaco go on multiplying. The clever German writer, Hans Wachenhausen, has just published an account of the petty Principality, in which he mentions that the prince has sold out his interest in the gaming tables, receiving 8,500,000F. in lieu of an annuity of 650,000F. The inference drawn is that he sees the system too monstrous to last.'

A few days later *La Colonie Etrangère* of Nice commented with some smugness:

'Neighbouring and distant populations are stirring more and more. They see with disquietude the existence of public gaming tables at Monaco, and desire their abolition, for they daily fear their pernicious consequences. They demand that this scene of shame and debauchery should disappear as speedily as possible, so that foreigners may no longer be deterred from visiting the charming sites of Nice and Menton. They demand that the French flag should no longer screen such an infamy, and that the vassal of France should be forced to introduce French laws on morality and decency into his petty state.'

Less than a month afterwards *Opinione* of Rome asked whether

'. . . if the Prince of Monaco, with the simple view of increasing his income, were to take into his employ a crew of pirates, who should spread terror along the Mediterranean coast, or a band of brigands, threatening the roads communicating between Italy and France, those states would look on such a condition of things, because Monaco was a free and independent country;

or would it not rather be their duty to interfere at once and employ all means for safeguarding their subjects? The ever-increasing evil at Monte Carlo should be removed without delay. . . .

'All nations have manifested their indignation against this horrible social plague. What nation is there that has not suffered through it in the persons of some of its children? Italy has certainly suffered more than all, as the statistics of suicide certainly prove!'

The Pope himself received a deputation from an organization whose sources of finance were not far removed from the municipality of Nice, which called itself the Committee for the Suppression of Gambling at Monte Carlo.

'I am informed that His Holiness [*The Times*'s Rome correspondent cabled to London], deeply deploring the lamentable effects of the gaming tables there, said that, in the presence of so many fatal consequences, he could not do less than express his disapproval of the impunity granted to a system of gambling which was the cause of so many suicides, of the ruin of so many families, of the loss of so many souls.'

The Times repeated the headline: 'THE MONTE CARLO SCANDAL' and reported:

'Whenever Monte Carlo feels itself in danger, it endeavours to effect a diversion. The device for acting on French susceptibilities is to represent that Germany or America has an idea of buying the Principality, the intended moral being that the Monaco kinglet must not be driven to desperation by attacks on the gambling system which supplies its revenue.

'The same trick is now being resorted to in order to discourage the Italian movement against the scandal. A Roman newspaper professes to have received a telegram from Paris, according to which a concession for a rival gaming table outside the confines of Monaco is contemplated.

'It need hardly be said that this is a pure invention. The French Government would not dream of authorising such an establishment, and indeed it would be absolutely illegal. This is a specimen of the shifts to which Monte Carlo is reduced.'

The shift to which Monte Carlo, or rather M. Blanc, was reduced in reality was somewhat different. He paid the civic leaders of Nice and the local bishop 300,000 francs a year between them to cease their campaign against the casino, which they promptly did. Stopping the voicing of public indignation was not so easy, however. Queen Victoria showed her disapproval by refusing to call on Prince Charles, or even to receive him, while she was passing through Monaco. The King of Württemberg, who seems to have entertained ideas that the whole affair might culminate in the European powers' removing Charles from his little throne and placing himself upon it, ostentatiously called for a copy of a book called *The Scandal of Monte Carlo*

The Last Train from Monte Carlo, by A. Castaigne, 1904.

to be delivered to his villa in Nice. The press of Britain, France, Germany, Italy and Russia continued to inveigh against the principality, and eventually and inevitably the uncontrollable campaign rebounded against Nice itself.

In point of fact, while the civic fathers of Nice had been leading the clamour against the iniquitous policy of Monaco to permit gambling more than fifteen illegal casinos had been operating in their own town, run not by a respectable figure like M. Blanc but by members of the underworld, under the covert but benign protection of the municipality and the local police. M. Levaillant, director of the Sûreté Publique, publicly censured Nice and other French resorts for their laxity over gaming, ordered that lists of all known operators of *salons des jeux* be sent to him so that prosecutions might be instituted and, in his own words, consented as a concession 'to allow, as a simple amusement, the game of *petits chevaux*, on condition that the stake never exceeds the sum of two francs. It is important that you see that this condition is not evaded in any way. Every infraction of this rule is to be immediately reported to me.'

In cracking down on gambling M. Levaillant could not realistically have hoped to succeed, and he did not. In conferring on Nice the reputation of a seamy town where no gentleman would be seen himself, let alone permit his wife or daughters to visit it, he achieved much. Monte Carlo then administered a *coup de grâce* by engineering press reports that Nice was in the grip of a cholera epidemic.

'It is really distressing to think how impotent the honest side of the European press proves itself to be in contradicting the infamous lying press [wrote a correspondent in Nice to *Travel and Talk*]. The Swiss and Italian newspapers continue publishing, even now, that from 20 to 40 persons die every day of *Asiatic* cholera in Nice! An Italian gentleman called on me yesterday, stating that Milan and Genoa were full of visitors waiting for the deathly epidemic at Nice to disappear, and that at one hotel in Mentone, he was told the same thing!

'You will really do a great service to the honest working classes of Nice if you can counteract in your useful and independent journal the infamous lies that are being circulated by interested persons. The interested persons who circulate these reports seek to profit by the misfortunes they inflict on others, because it seems that in love, war, elections and *business* all is to be considered fair.

'A few courageous visitors have arrived here with a little fear and trembling at first, but they are pleased to have proved themselves braver than their fellow-travellers. Mr Harris, the worthy British consul here, and many other influential inhabitants of Nice do all they can to make the actual truth known, but their endeavours seem to be powerless against the prevalent cholera scare.'

The winter season of 1882 and 1883 was a disastrous one for the resort. From Monte Carlo Mr Aubrey de Vere Beauclerk wrote to *The Times*: 'This place is pretty full . . . some thirty or forty new villas have been built, furnished and occupied here since March. These villas are not run-up buildings such as we are accustomed to in England, but all well built of blocks of beautiful white freestone with staircases and balconies of marble.'

Meanwhile, it was reported from Nice that it was '. . . extraordinarily empty. At some of the best hotels there are only two or three families, and I hear of some smaller ones thinking of closing altogether.

'Whereas villas and apartments used to be let for six months from October to April, the season is now reduced to the short interval between the races in January and the regatta in March. Most of the hotels do not open until November 15, the promenades are deserted until the end of December, villas are let by the month, and most of them remain empty six or eight weeks, the letting of one being considered a piece of good fortune.

'The artisans are in great distress, bankruptcies are twice as numerous as in the rest of France, four out of the six stockbrokers are bankrupt or under prosecution, the house-owners have a very gloomy prospect, and the Crédit Foncier is obliged to wait for the interest on most of its mortgages, as foreclosure would be still worse for it.'

But, the article ended, whistling to the wind, 'everything tends to show that it is Monte Carlo which is tottering and that one more resolute effort will suffice to overthrow it'.

In his inaugural address that winter the president of the Nice chamber of commerce attributed 80 per cent of the town's bankruptcies to 'gambling losses in clubs – alas! too numerous – or in places which shall remain nameless'. The simpler truth was that Monte Carlo had taken on Nice in a battle for the title of the Riviera's premier resort, and had won handsomely, however foully.

It was Nagelmackers, with his Train Bleu, who came to the town's rescue. He persuaded the city fathers to launch a *grande*

SOUVENIR DE MONTE - CARLO. „RIEN NE VA PLUS!"

A satirical picture postcard from Monte Carlo.

exposition to coincide with the inauguration of his splendid express, and to present a new face for Nice to the world. Throughout the summer the town's artisans and twenty thousand migrant labourers worked to transform the town. Its notorious sewers, which had previously disgorged straight into the sea, in many cases opposite the hotels on the Promenade des Anglais, were rebuilt and brought into conformity with the then most advanced ideas on hygiene.

A municipal casino – without *salles des jeux* – was constructed at a cost of £240,000. 'Like every undertaking in Nice, the enterprise was assailed during its progress by fierce, and it may be said, factious opposition. So high do party politics run here, that they produce absolute blindness to the public interest.' So Opper de Blowitz reported to *The Times*. But for him, he was surprisingly complimentary about the outcome.

'The building is constructed on a long and solid bridge over the River Paillon, the dry and unwholesome bed of which will, when the scheme is completed, be almost hidden from view. A fine open space in front of the casino, by which the Place Massena is doubled in size, is not the least of the advantages conferred by the work. . . . The principal facade of the casino, which looks southwards, facing the sea, is somewhat squat with no claims to architectural beauty. So little does it augur for the interior of the building, that one feels surprise on entering the rectangular winter garden, quite a gem in its way, in which gigantic palm trees and a small forest of exotic plants spread their graceful forms over undulating grass plots. A miniature lake and grass walks are laid out under the glass roof, so high that air and space may be said to be the characteristics. The café and restaurants stretching along one side will doubtless soon be in high favour with visitors, and the little shops of the other side impart an animation to the scene.'

A 'charming little theatre' with a thousand seats adjoined, where a season of Italian opera would be held each year; and to the front of the building was a suite of rooms to accommodate the town's most fashionable club, the Masséna.

It was indeed a new beginning to the town's fortunes. The Train Bleu began its run once a week, and then three times a week and soon, daily. The war of attrition with Monaco was forgotten. 'Magnificent new houses on the boulevards of Longchamps and La Bouffa seem to be filled as fast as they are finished,' said one contemporary account. 'The increase in first-class houses let off in spacious apartments is extraordinary; new hotels are being opened by the score.'

Queen Victoria moved her winter court from Hyères to Cimiez, the English quarter of Nice. Herr and Frau Steinbruch's Hotel d'Angleterre not only returned to its old self but flourished as never before, counting among its guests the Duke of Edinburgh, Prince and Princess Christian, Princess Louise and the Marquess of Lorne, while the Dukes and Duchesses of Albany, Argyll, Marlborough, Sutherland and Westminster all gathered there.

The Train Bleu also brought to Nice large numbers of middle-class people, who now had the means to winter in the south. All that was needed to complete the scene was a truly grand hotel. This, of course, Nagelmackers provided, in the Riviera Palace, set in its own vast gardens. Nagelmackers claimed that it was a self-contained resort, independent of the city itself for facilities for amusement. The most convincing tribute to its luxury was that Queen Victoria was so impressed that she moved out of her own villa at Cimiez into an apartment in the hotel.

It is worth giving some account here of Her Majesty's annual progress to the Riveria. Her private coach was attached to one of Nagelmackers's trains at Cherbourg, and she travelled over the next twenty hours or so in the train, arriving without a hint of exhaustion after nine o'clock. On her arrival she found that the mayor and prefect had conceded to her request for a minimum of ceremony. They greeted her with brief speeches of welcome, and she boarded her landau to take her to the hotel.

'Directly her Majesty had left the station [*American Society* magazine reported] there was a rush of well-dressed people to the large waiting-room, the floor of which had been strewn with blue violets. Over these large blossoms the Queen had stepped as lightly as possible, in order not to bruise the flowers of which she is so fond. The porters would have swept the whole floral carpet away but for the invasion of the crowd, who gathered up alike the violets which were crushed and those which had not been trodden on, bearing them off as souvenirs of the occasion.

Reaching the hotel, 'scarcely had she been conducted to her dressing room ere she inquired for the menu of that night's dinner. Like all her family, the Queen enjoys her food and eats plenty of it. The "card", beautifully printed in gold, surmounted by the Royal arms, was at once brought to Her Majesty, who was pleased to signify her complete approval of the arrangement.

PERSONALITIES ON THE RIVIERA.

THE DUCHESS OF SUTHERLAND,

who is now enjoying the Carnival Season at Mentone. She is an accomplished novelist and playwright, and is now busily engaged upon a Book of Travel.

LORD GRENFELL,

recently in Command of the 4th Army Corps, in uniform as Colonel of the King's Royal Rifles. He is at present taking a holiday at Nice.

LADY MARY DAWSON,

the youngest daughter of the Earl and Countess of Dartrey, also staying at Nice. She is returning early in April to act as bridesmaid in the Stafford-Butler wedding.

"LES AMATEURS DU SPORT."

LORD DECIES,

now engaged in a Polo Tournament at Cannes. He is a famous soldier, rider to hounds, and cricketer. In addition he owns several racehorses.

THE DUCHESS OF BEDFORD,

in the coverts calling to her dogs. Her devotion to fishing, hunting, and shooting, marks her as a real "Sporting Duchess." She is at present staying at Vernet-les-Bains.

THE EARL OF ROSSLYN,

here represented with his favourite dog. He is making a cruise to Morocco and Madeira and will not return until April.

'Considering that the meal was not served until eleven o'clock, the menu was a rather formidable one, consisting as it did of the following dishes: two soups (*crème d'orge* and *Princesse*), filets of whiting *au gratin*, fried smelts, saddle of mutton, croquettes of chicken in the "Richelieu" style, sweetbreads with French beans and peas, roasted capons, asparagus, *soufflé* of pineapple and dessert.

'Lunch, and a substantial lunch too, had been served that day in the train between one and two o'clock; the famous copper tea kettle which has been on so many journeys with Her Majesty and her youngest daughter, was requisitioned at six, and Princess Beatrice presided, as usual, over the tea-table; and even after that there was *quelque chose à goûter* before the illustrious travellers sat down to the uncommonly festive board at the hotel!

'It should be understood that when the Queen is on her travels considerably less ceremonial is observed than when the Court is in England or Scotland. On this particular Monday night, the ladies and gentlemen of the suite dined with the Queen, and Her Majesty, who had slept better than usual on the train, was as chatty as the youngest present. That is saying a great deal, for everybody knows what a lively conversationalist Princess "Trixy" is, and what a lot of funny things she has to gossip about when not frozen by the Royal etiquette from which she so seldom escapes when at home.

'Midnight had sounded before the dessert was put on, or rather, I should say before it was attacked, for the grapes, oranges and strawberries (at a guinea a pound) were displayed on the table all through the meal. The Queen is and always has been most abstemious in the matter of wine and spirits, seldom touching champagne, but enjoying an occasional glass all the same, especially when it is so old and dry that ordinary people would not care to drink it. Some special Burgundy proved greatly to Her Majesty's taste, and she retired to rest expressing her delight at the arrangements which had been made for her comfort.'

The second hotel that Nagelmackers built on the Riviera, at La Turbie, was more magnificent still, having even its private railway line from Monaco Station, where clients entrusted their baggage to the hotel staff, boarded the little train and travelled 1500 feet up the hill, to come to a halt in the olive grove facing the hotel's entrance.

'At the first sight of the fairy palace which dominates Monte Carlo, one is tempted to construct some kind of romance about its inception and execution. Let us indulge that fancy [bubbled one of Nagelmackers's copywriters]. One afternoon, four or so years ago, a man of business, with artistic instincts, was strolling on the hillside at Monte Carlo. He knew the place well, but his eye roved over the exquisite prospect with a new appreciation

OPPOSITE A profile of British aristocrats who arrived on the Riviera on the Train Bleu, 1912.

La Turbie.

THIS lovely spot, rightly termed the "Winter Righi," has now been brought, like its Swiss prototype, into quick communication with lower levels by means of a cog-wheel railway. The Restaurant at the summit, to which is attached a small Hotel, is under the direction of those famous Restaurateurs M. M. Noël and Pattard, and forms a convenient rendezvous for those who undertake the delightful excursion. The journey, in luxuriously fitted train, occupies only twenty-five minutes from the station at Monte Carlo, although La Turbie is 1,500 feet above the level of the sea. A series of enchanting views unfold themselves as the train rises, each more beautiful than the other, until the summit is reached. From there the view embraces, as in a map spread out before one, the whole of the principality of Monaco, Cap Martin, Mentone, Bordighera, San Remo, Corsica, &c., &c., while to breathe the mountain air for a few hours forms one of the delights of a séjour at Monte Carlo. A new station has been built in the olive garden at the terrace entrance of the Riviera Palace Hotel at Monte Carlo Supérieur for the convenience of visitors at that palatial establishment.

London Office of the Company:

14, COCKSPUR STREET.

of its beauties. Below him, the terraces of the Casino glittered in the sun. A miniature fleet lay in the dainty bay of Monaco. Away to the left Cap Martin baked in the haze and Bordighera summoned thoughts of Italy. But the man of business refused to think of Italy except as a scenic accessory to the scheme which had suddenly taken shape in his mind.

'He eyed the hillside in a very determined manner, and felt in his pocket for a pencil. In a few moments, the pencil had

OPPOSITE An advertisement for Nagelmackers's hotel, the Riviera Palace in La Turbie. BELOW Queen Victoria breakfasting *en famille* in Nice, where she regularly wintered.

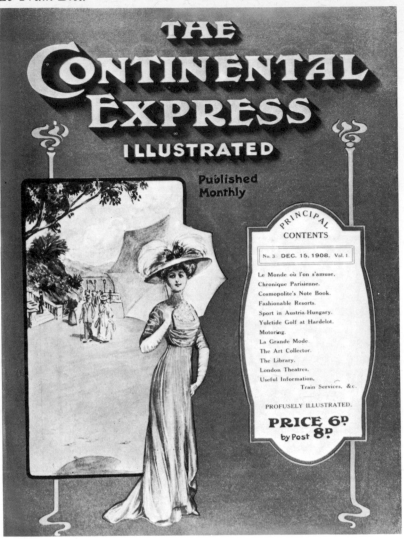

The cover of *The Continental Express*, 1908.

sketched a plan which took the greatest liberties with the hill, scooped a large piece out of it, made a plateau rich with olive and orange groves, and erected a stately building. Since Aladdin, no architect had worked at such a speed!

'It was a plan for a new hotel in a situation unsurpassed on this lovely coast. "Here," thought the pioneer, "here at last is the ideal site. There is no finer view in the Riviera. The air is superb; the access is easy. Ha! First of all I will secure the ground so that unsuspecting gossip hereabouts may think I want to live like a landed proprietor upon a charming estate.

'The first task was to lay out the garden. In the Riviera a garden is more Aladdin-like in the spontaneity and swiftness of its growth than any other handiwork of man. Everything springs to bloom in this climate with the sheer rapture of living.

Begun in 1897, the Botanic Garden of the Riviera Palace is now in a perfection.

'Provision is made too for indoor exercise by the immense Hall and Winter Garden, with about two thousand square yards under cover.

'Of the hotel, the first point in the design was to give every room a southerly aspect. Then of the 150 visitors' rooms (exclusive of the quarter for servants) at least 75 have salons, dressing rooms and bathrooms attached. A great improvement has been effected in the service. With the best organisation there is always something defective in the system which compels the visitor to summon servants to his room. When he has found the bell, he has to master the printed instructions, often in primitive English, such as "One strike for the woman of chamber, two strike for the butler" and so on. The chances are that he bungles the "strike" which, after an exasperating interval, brings the wrong person, who is overwhelmed with unmerited reproaches and retires with a sense of injury.

'What could be simpler [the brochure boasted] than an improved telephonic apparatus by which orders are communicated direct to the various offices without sending for the servant at all?

'Further guarantees of celerity are provided by three electric passenger lifts. An even more important assurance of comfort is the heating of the building by steam, a very different method from that of circulating hot air which impairs the vitality and increases the risks of catching chills.'

Thus equipped to be the two focal points of the Riviera, Nice and Monte Carlo ceased to be squabbling sisters and became the coast's twin queens. Nagelmackers launched one new train after another to take the leisured classes there each winter – from St Petersburg, Berlin, Hamburg, Amsterdam, Vienna, Rome, Budapest. A typical season was vividly described by Nagelmackers's *Traveller de Luxe*, poignantly soon before the First World War broke out:

'Wealthy Hungarians, Rumanians and Russians, who usually arrive early to escape their own rigorous climates are few and far between. But the English contingent is cheerful and numerous, well provided mostly with handsome furs and canine pets. Bringing the latter out is easy, but how about the poor darlings' six months' quarantine in the spring? Fox terriers, alert and frisky, seem to have invaded Nice.

'The fact is that all along the coast in late November, the early birds arrive, a fairly fine flock, and they settle in groups here and there – harbingers of the great rush later. But there is always a lull – Germans and English like to keep Christmas at home, and parents wait till after the holidays before disporting themselves in the sunny south.

'But then there are also the indolent few who shirk the really hard work of Christmas shopping, and thinking out of presents and charities, or who have few home ties, and prefer the very real gaiety and sumptuous fare given by all the Hotels here, with plum puddings, laboriously made with English receipts, and with genuine mince pies to follow. The only difficulty is to pick one's way through the long and tempting menu, and to leave a vacant corner for the English dishes. So just before the 25th, the Omnibuses came rattling along, piled high with trunks, and there were wreathed smiles from the open portals. Soon after January 15th, the fun grows fast and furious, the difficulty is to house everyone.

'As becomes a capital of pleasure, Nice is the first to bristle into the activity of fêtes. This is a matter in which she does her duty nobly. Sunday the 8th, therefore, was a day of much music. All the trading community subscribe liberally. Every brass band that can be collected comes and marches and plays, first altogether, for a grand concert on the Place Massena, and then separately in various quarters.

'In the evening, there was a *Retraite aux Flambeaux*, in which the gallant little Chasseurs Alpins (they are picked small men for climbing, as lithe and wiry as cats, and know every stone and cranny on the frontier Alps) in blue, with beret pulled rakishly well over the left eye, vied with the taller linemen, "the Red Legs", in scarlet trousers, in blowing down the civilian bandsmen by the light of their picturesque flaming torches. Proceedings wound up with a ball at the casino, to which foreign residents and habitués were invited and went.

'This fête, inaugurated by the townspeople, is now looked upon as the official opening of the season.

'I said there were few Russians in Nice, but as a matter of fact there were enough to organise a charming charity show the other day, at the Astoria. It began with a concert, the prelude of theatricals, ending with a dance with cotillon, besides minor attractions. . . .

'The Baron and Baronne de Meyrennet have returned. This means that things will go merrily at the very exclusive and fashionable country club which is in the grounds of the great rotunda of the Hotel Impériale, one of the most comfortable existing.

'Of the making of hotels, it seems there is no end. But as all the world sooner or later is irresistibly bound to gravitate hither, apparently they are but supplying a necessity. It was my privilege to inspect the Halls of light and beauty in the big new Palace, with an arresting dome, that has now risen on the Promenade des Anglais, and is due to the genius and enterprise of M. Negresco. The amount of invention, thought and ingenuity, coupled with art, that he puts into the construction of a modern Caravanserai of luxury and refinement brought to its highest pitch, is truly astounding. We are always hearing of the "last

word" in hotel perfection – Monsieur Negresco seems really to point to finality in this generation at any rate. . . .

'At the Casino, apart from the inevitable "flutter" there is an admirable theatrical programme doing the greatest honour by its variety and excellent troupe to the able director M. Farconnet, such stars as Mesdames Bartet, Marie Lecomte and Galipeaux will be seen. The Theatre of Nice can vie with many a Paris one. Then it is a pleasant place to dine and saunter into stall or box after. And Theatre Suppers are not liable to be finished in darkness as in London.

'A miniature bronze replica of the poetic and beautiful statue of Queen Victoria is being made. A deputation will go to London, probably next May, to present it to King George. It will be pleasant to hear of some return of the lavish hospitality shown to the English here when the unveiling of the statue took place at Cimiez, as the close of the *Entente Cordiale* fêtes. . . .

'Villas are letting fast, and that guide, philosopher and friend of all travellers, Mr. Waight of Johnson Riviera Agency, Nice, is extremely busy relieving all and sundry of all care and trouble for stays long and short.'

After the war it was the turn of the Americans to take over the French Riviera as their summer resort. It was the era of the Murphys, the Hemingways, the Fitzgeralds and the Duncans. It is a world described in *Tender is the Night*; and perhaps the change of character the Côte d'Azur underwent is most succinctly described by Calvin Tomkins, in his account of life in Antibes between the wars:

'The Murphys gave a party at the Villa America. . . . Fitzgerald again seemed to be under some compulsion to spoil the evening. He started things off inauspiciously by walking up to one of the guests, a young writer, and asking him in a loud, jocular tone whether he was a homosexual. The man quietly said "Yes" and Fitzgerald retreated in temporary embarrassment. When dessert came, Fitzgerald picked a fig from a bowl of pineapple sherbert and threw it at the Princess de Caraman-Chimay, a house guest of the Murphys' friend and neighbour, the Princesse de Poix. It hit her between the shoulder blades. She stiffened for a moment and then went on talking as if nothing had happened. At this point, MacLeish took Fitzgerald aside, suggested that he behave himself, and received for his pains, without warning, a roundhouse right to the jaw. Then Fitzgerald, apparently feeling that still not enough attention was being paid to him, began throwing Sarah's gold-flecked Venetian wine glasses over the garden wall. He had smashed three of them this way before Gerald stopped him. As the party was breaking up, Gerald went up to Scott (among the last to leave) and told him that he would not be welcome in his house for three weeks, a term of banishment that was observed to the day.'

Monte Carlo was famed for its pigeon shooting: a poster advertising a shoot.

8. Travelling Like a Sahib

Europeans travelling on Indian railways took with them a bevy of servants rather than rely on those provided by the railway administration.

An overland route to India had been dreamt of – even planned in some detail – for at least two centuries before railways came into being; and it was probably the greatest entrepreneurial setback in Nagelmackers's life that international diplomacy and the mutual suspicions of the countries involved frustrated him from building such a line from Constantinople eastwards.

In the event, however, much to the dismay of the English, who felt a God-given right to carry out the work themselves, the Germans constructed a railway eastwards from the Turkish capital through Baghdad to Basra on the Arabian Gulf. As a result, it became possible soon after the beginning of the twentieth century to travel by train from London to the Arabian Gulf – some two-thirds of the way to Bombay – and a growing number of English tourists began to holiday in India. They came in sufficient numbers, indeed, for Thomas Cook and Sons' Bombay office to offer a choice of over a dozen escorted rail tours round India. Travel was first class throughout. Overnight accommodation was generally in retiring rooms for European passengers provided by the railway administration for 1 rupee per night, which Cooks held to be immaculately clean and more comfortable than many high-class European hotels.

But above all, India was a country for the individual traveller. Many moved about in specially rented private carriages, which were available for the modest sum of eight full fares per journey. These were extraordinary, two-storey structures – the kitchen and servants' quarters below, the sahib's bedroom, sitting room, dining room and bathroom on the upper floor.

One might ask why a visiting sahib had need of such space when ordinary first-class compartments, more roomy than European ones, well-furnished with leather armchairs, tables and green sunshields that could be let down when the light became too intense, were also available.

'Journeys are somewhat elaborate proceedings [Sidney Low explained in 1905], not to be transacted in the casual fashion customary in the Outer World.

'It is no case of packing a portmanteau, whistling at the door for a hansom, arriving at the station ten minutes before the train starts, giving a sixpence to a civil porter and finding yourself under way with an open magazine upon your knees. There are no hansoms; and if there were, a file of them would be needed to transport a very ordinary Sahib's effects. The amount of luggage which people take with them, even on comparatively short journeys, would amaze those austere travellers who believe that one trunk and a handbag should be enough to carry them anywhere. This may be sound reasoning in Europe, but it certainly does not apply in India.'

The first necessity, on arrival in Bombay, was to purchase one's own bedding. No respectable traveller in India slept in

any but his own, and everywhere he went a large canvas bag containing a rolled-up mattress, sheets, pillows and two sets of blankets – one thick and one thin – went with him. Another necessary purchase was a metal and glass camp lantern with a large paraffin reservoir, contained in a tin box – electricity supplies were not to be counted upon up-country. And although all the major trains had commodious restaurant cars where both western and oriental meals were available at modest cost and in great quantity, and although most stations also had refreshment rooms, few ventured forth from Bombay without a tiffin box to supply between-meal snacks: the contents of such a box comprised a teapot, cups, saucers, plates and spoons, some bottles of soda water, a tin of biscuits and a pot of marmalade.

The wardrobe of a European traveller in India was more extensive by far than that of someone merely wintering in the south of France, or touring the spas of Eastern Europe. To allow for all contingencies, a man took with him several light flannel suits to wear during the heat of the day, and heavier wear for the evenings and mornings. 'Madras rig' – patent

The palatial headquarters of the B. B. & C. I. Railway in Bombay. Indian railways established a grandeur unrivalled in the rest of the world.

153

"Trekking" Accessories for Tropical Climes.

An iceless cocktail shaker: worked with a special freezing mixture, this "Igene" cocktail shaker keeps the contents icy cold for an hour. It is obtainable rom Farrow and Jackson's, 8, Haymarket, S.W.

A portable fan worked by paraffin: the "Ky-Ko" fan, from Humphreys and Crook, needs no electricity to create a constant breeze, and will run all night without attention.

Music wherever you go: a light self-contained H.M.V. gramophone which will withstand excessive heat and hard travel. There is room in the lid to carry six records.

A watch protected from climatic changes: the Ermeto watch, with a sliding case which keeps it unaffected by dust, dampness, and heat. From De Trevars, of 197a, Regent Street, W.

A collapsible wardrobe for trekking: this ingenious affair folds up quite flat, and the mirror can be taken out and set up on a temporary dressing table. From Humphreys and Crook, 3, Haymarket, S.W.

Civilisation wherever you go: no matter how vast the distances, the marvellous new Selector three-valve wireless set will record music and speech at full loudspeaker strength from practically every country in the world.

The "movie" companion who never fails: this light, compact Cine Kodak will take moving pictures anywhere, making a wonderful record of all your travels.

A torch requiring no batteries: this "No-Battery" electric torch is self-generating, and is guaranteed for twelve months. Either a spotlight or floodlight is obtainable.

Olive Hewerdine

leather shoes, black silk trousers, maroon silk cummerbund, white silk shirt and black bow tie – had yet to become acceptable attire for dinner parties, and it was necessary to take with one a complete assortment of tail coats, white and black tie ensembles and, if appropriate, regimental dress uniform, to meet the demands of hospitality during breaks in the journey. As for women, Bradshaw's guide for British visitors to India devoted three pages to a list of the components of the minimal amount of clothing to be taken with one.

It was also *de rigueur* not to leave Bombay without a couple of saddles and bridles, riding breeches, boots, leggings, spurs and whips, for riding was a common form of hospitality. Similarly, it would be a man unconcerned with the niceties of Anglo-Indian life who ventured into the sub-continent without a couple of shotguns, a sporting rifle and ample ammunition.

All these appurtenances and more – such as a portable bureau containing the wherewithal to write letters – were necessary for the individual rail traveller in India because few hotels existed outside the principal cities; and the Anglo-Indian community, thrust inwards upon itself in club and on polo ground, welcomed lone English visitors of good standing as heartily as they loathed the sight-seeing incursions of Thomas Cook's groups of 'white barbarians'. A courtesy call to sign the book at the British residency, and the invitations to dinner, to join

OPPOSITE Some of the products which ensured that British travellers maintained the style to which they were accustomed.

BELOW An advertisement for a luxury travel case.

J·C· VICKERY·

179·181·183 REGENT ST. LONDON ·W·

Their Majesties Jeweller, Silversmith & Dressing Case Manufacturer

HIGHEST QUALITY.

GOOD VALUE.

By Appointment to T.M. the King and Queen.

VICKERY'S FOR TRAVEL AND MOTOR REQUISITES, LUNCHEON CASES, LEATHER GOODS OF ALL KINDS, SILVERWARE, JEWELLERY, &c., &c.

Inspection invited, or illustrations and prices of any requirements sent on application.

A very smart 20 in. Green or Blue Morocco Dressing Case, with beautiful Engine-turned Sterling Silver Fittings, latest design, only **£25**; very special value. Other designs, fitted Gold, Silver, Tortoiseshell, Ivory, &c., **£10** to **£300**.

hunting parties, to go pig-sticking, to become an honorary member of the club, would flock to one at the station rest room.

But that was not all that was required. A folding chair and table, a cigar humidor, a leather case containing a supply of whisky and glasses, a portable library, a mahogany camera and stand and other comforts were normally added as well. Indeed, almost the only thing the traveller did not require to take with him was money. India was the home of the chit – so one commodity one did not have to take was money. You signed for everything from a private railway carriage to a sixteen anna cigar and glass of soda water.

On arrival in Bombay, you presented yourself, together with a letter of introduction from your bank, at Kings and Kings or one of the other financial agencies, who in turn gave you a letter establishing your credit with them from the Himalayan foothills to Ceylon. It was, in effect, the precursor of today's credit card, although more widely valid; and as some travellers complain today, so then was cash positively discouraged in transactions with hoteliers and others. (The fear was, of course, that the servants would pocket it, whereas a chit drawn on Kings and Kings was of no use to them.)

Even small change for tips was unnecessary – one's servant kept the petty cash and handed it out where appropriate, rendering occasional accounts of a meticulous but linguistically obscure nature. This brings one to the subject of travellers' servants.

In India, as in Europe, the coming of luxurious trains had created the traveller's servant as a new occupation. In Europe, they advertised their services in the personal column of *The Times* and the like, emphasizing their knowledge of languages and their familiarity, not only with the functions required of a valet or a lady's maid, but also with specific regions. At the port of Bombay, as a P & O or British India steamship came in, European passengers would be besieged as they walked down the gangplank by Indian bearers offering their services throughout a tour of the country. All were able to proffer references written in English, and many, illiterate in English, had failed to take the precaution of having them translated before proffering them. Thus a beaming supplicant would thrust upon a new arrival a testament to his slovenliness, laziness and dishonesty. The wise traveller passed them by, and hired his servant through his banker's Bombay agents.

During a rail tour of India, it was the servant's task to go to the station ahead of his master, with a bullock cart or, if need be, an elephant-drawn lorry, containing the baggage, and supervise its loading on to the train. A small regiment of porters would be enlisted to effect this, it being the etiquette for each one to handle only a single piece of baggage, whether it be a portmanteau or a fishing rod.

An English picnic in
India.

At the appointed hour, the sahib and the memsahib presented
themselves at the station to be greeted by the stationmaster,
who presented them with the chit for the porters' tip to sign;
then they boarded their private carriage.

During the journey, the servant brought tea or whisky-and-
soda at appropriate times and intervals, told them of impending
meal stops and guarded their carriage while they ate. Even if
the train had its own dining car the private carriages meant
there were no corridors, so it was necessary for a stop to be
made to enable passengers to alight from their own accommoda-
tions and board another coach in which to eat, the train stopping
again when their meal was finished to allow them to return.

At night the servant made up the beds, served the evening
whisky; and in the morning, brought the *chotta hazri* – pre-
breakfast tea and toast. He also gave advance warning of any
interesting sights along the way, was responsible for handing
out gratuities from the fund of petty cash in his care, and
generally smoothed the visitor's path.

Of all the modern railway journeys I have undertaken – from
London to Moscow, from Danzig on the Baltic across Europe
to Varna on the Black Sea, from Chiang Mai to Bangkok – the
most memorable by far was one I made in 1966 in India, from
Delhi to Jammu in the north. It was so because it was so un-
modern. The 'Rheingold' may offer radio telephone, multi-
lingual secretarial facilities and a barber's shop. The Japanese

157

'Bullet' may be the last word in 'airline-style luxury'. But the Kashmir Express offers a glimpse, albeit a faded one, of what it was like to be a visiting English sahib touring India by rail in the heyday of the Raj.

We arrived, two fellow-journalists and myself, at Delhi Station, to find the place in a state of seemingly total confusion. It is not the custom to travel light, and the platforms were piled high with baggage. Nor is it the practice to depart without being seen off by a suitable retinue of perhaps a dozen friends or relatives. Movement around the baggage piles and through the crowds was nearly impossible.

We were promptly spotted, because of our white faces, as the innocents we were, and taken into the hands of a railway official. He kindly helped us to hire bedding for the journey – a thin mattress, sheets, blankets, pillows, towel. Then he proposed that he should help us hire a servant for the journey. A servant? He explained that it was *de rigueur* for foreigners in India. A servant was duly hired from one of a crowd standing on the platform.

He showed us to our compartment – vast, teak-panelled with brocade curtains. He made up our beds, disappeared and returned with tea made with condensed milk. Throughout the journey, he reappeared at regular intervals to bring us more tea, soda water and beer. Where he spent the rest of the time we never established. In the morning more tea was brought, the bedding was removed and the compartment was converted into a day saloon. Then the train drew up at a country station. A solitary table stood on the platform, covered in a white cloth with three chairs round it. To this we were led, and were seated. A white-gowned waiter appeared and served us a breakfast of boiled eggs and toast, which we ate under the fascinated gaze of a crowd of locals who had gathered, apparently on their way to work.

The day passed in a leisurely manner, at a speed of twenty miles an hour or so. As a correspondent had written to the *Manchester Guardian* over half a century before: 'Government railways in India have their own notions of propriety, and scorn the indecorous haste of private enterprise.' The son of a judge, travelling from university to visit his parents in Jammu, introduced himself and engaged us in polite conversation about Sir Winston Churchill as a war leader and the insights gained into everyday English life from an extensive and devoted study of the novels of P.G.Wodehouse.

At first, when we drew into a station to find a crowd of uniformed schoolchildren on the platform, we took this to be coincidence, along with the fact that they soon found the window of our compartment and gathered round, staring, pointing and giggling at us. After perhaps three or four stations we began to tire of the repeated experience, and before the train drew into the next took the precaution of pulling our curtains.

We had hardly been stopped for five minutes when we heard commotion and a loud exchange between railway officials. Our Indian travelling companion left the compartment to investigate, and returned to ask if we would mind if he drew back the curtains. Not wishing to carry discourtesy too far, we agreed. He drew the curtains back and we were confronted again by another sea of turbanned boys' faces staring at us. We bore the inspection with a little noticeable irritation. But as the train drew out the Indian with us appealed to our indulgence and forbearance. Children in that part of the world, he explained, had never seen white people before; and stationmasters were alerting their colleagues in succession up the line to our impending arrival, so that the local school could be advised and the classes turned out to undertake, with ourselves as subjects, some elementary fieldwork into what their one-time rulers had actually looked like.

Towards lunchtime the servant appeared and inquired whether we wished a European or a 'Hindu military' meal – the latter term meaning a meat rather than the more usual vegetarian curry. Our orders were written down, wrapped round a stone and thrown out at the next signal box we passed. And so we drew into the next station to find another white-clothed table laid on the platform awaiting us.

At journey's end we paid off our servant – about £2 for some thirty hours' attendance and, needless to say, double the standard rate. He accepted it with that coolness that always indicates that one has grossly overpaid, and found us a taxi to take us to the government bungalow.

Tourists did not go to India only to admire the Red Fort and the Taj Mahal, or even the trappings of empire, such as Lutyens's magnificent Janpath in the new capital. The prospect of hunting drew visitors from the western world; and the railway administration catered to them imaginatively by having built and providing mobile shooting boxes. These, like the special cars that could be attached to a train in return for eight first-class fares, were two-storey affairs, and still larger, to facilitate longer residence.

Arriving at Madras from Victoria Station, Bombay, on the twenty-five-miles-an-hour 'mail express', one called on the stationmaster, handed over one's chit, loaded one's luggage (as described above) into a box car, and oneself, one's companions and servants on to the shooting box. This would then be attached to a train going through the jungle, and uncoupled at any local station along the way one wished. Then it would often be shunted up a siding specially built to serve the needs of sportsmen, saving them as it did an arduous journey on foot to the lairs and watering places of the wild animals.

ABOVE Waiting for an Indian train! While English visitors toured the sub-continent in two-storeyed private carriages hauled by their own locomotives, the natives waited at stations, sometimes for more than a day for trains that were late.

I am indebted to 'Smooth-Bore', a Madras railway administration official who wrote a special pamphlet for visitors to India, published by the railway, for an account of the hunting that was thus enjoyed. Even for the Victorian English with their Scottish shooting estates, it was novel sport.

'The best time for ducks is during the months of December, January and February, after which they become unfit for the table. . . . Very often they choose a tank (artificial lake) covered in vegetation and rushes, generally very shallow, and then the sportsman has his skin or collapsible boat pushed along by coolies, when excellent sport is to be had, as the birds rise out of the long grass or weeds. . . . In very large tanks, it is a good plan to make many rafts covered with green boughs, and set them adrift three or four days before you intend to shoot the tank, and then have your own boat covered the same way, when you may drift down to within easy shot of the ducks, who have become accustomed to the rafts of similar appearance. It is by a

The Victoria Terminus Station, Bombay, the starting point for railway tours of the country.

contrivance similar to the above that the natives catch ducks in districts where the gunner has not penetrated. They procure a number of earthenware pots called chatties and set them afloat on a tank until the ducks have become used to them and then putting one of the chatties on his head a native walks into the tank, the chatty alone with hole for the eyes being visible. He is thus able to walk right amongst a flock of teal or duck and seizes one by the legs down under water and pops it into a net at his girdle, and thus procures a goodly number before the flock become suspicious.'

In weedy tanks 'Smooth-Bore' counselled that the native attendants should be discouraged from going in after the ducks, for fear of their being caught by the weeds and drowning, thus necessitating the sportsman to compensate their relatives.

He also prudently warned against paying beaters too much compensation should they be accidentally wounded by gunfire. The result, he said, was that on succeeding days other beaters would continually try to put themselves in the line of fire, so that they might collect too – on one memorable occasion in the Shevaroy Hills more beaters than game were bagged in the course of a day's shooting because of this.

The arrival of Lord Elgin, Viceroy of India, in his private train at Bruxor in the 1890s.

EXPOSITION UNIVERSELLE DE 1

COMPAGNIE INTER

AU

TRANSSIB

THÉÂTRE CHINOIS

Voyage de Moscou à Pékin

PANORAMA MOUVA

SERVICE DE RÉF

9. From Europe to Asia by *Train de Luxe*

…O

…TIONALE DES WAGONS-LITS

…OCADÉRO

…RIEN

RESTAURAN…

Moscovites

et

CHINOIS

dans

les gares

de

MOSCOU

et de

…DANS LE TRAIN DE LUXE

DE LA COMPAGNIE

The Trans-Siberian
Express was one of the
sensations of the Paris
Exhibition when it was
put on display there in
1900. Visitors ate in
stationary dining-cars
while a mammoth
tableau of Oriental
scenes moved past the
windows.

T he great sensation of the Paris Universal Exhibition of 1900 was Nagelmackers's Trans-Siberian International Express. He placed it on show in the Tuileries before putting it into service across Russia, to provide the first overland link between Western Europe and the Far East. It drew huge crowds and was awarded the gold medal; and no wonder. Nagelmackers's career as creator and pioneer of the *train de luxe* was one of repeatedly surpassing himself in his achievements. Now came his announcement that he was to provide not only the means of travelling to Peking, Shanghai, Seoul and even Tokyo in a fortnight by rail, but the possibility of doing so in conditions 'equal to the special trains reserved in Western Europe for the sole use of Royalty'.

Each of the coaches accommodated but eight people. Each two-berth coupé had a connecting *cabinet de toilette* and was decorated with the opulence of the *salon privé* of a St Petersburg merchant. Every carriage had its own drawing room and smoking room. One was decorated with white-lacquered limewood, mirrored walls, a ceiling frescoed with figures from Greek mythology and embroidered curtains. Another was in the style of Louis XVI, with bulging furniture of gold-embellished oak; a third was French Empire, and a fourth imperial Chinese.

The train had a library stocked with books in English, French, German and Russian, a glass-walled observation car and music room equipped with a full-sized grand piano, a hairdressing salon in white sycamore, a bathroom in green sycamore with a novel bath specially designed so that water could not spill out while the train was in motion, a gymnasium equipped with dumb-bells, exercise bicycle and rowing machine, and – although Nagelmackers had built both Catholic and Protestant churches along the route so that passengers might worship according to their custom during breaks in their journey – a chapel car. There was also a fully equipped darkroom for amateur photographers – though it is to be doubted whether this was provided for their convenience so much as for the tsarist censors, to whom undeveloped, exposed film in the possession of foreigners was as much anathema as it is to their Soviet successors.

The Siberian tundra was a terrain known to few but furtrapping nomads, mujiks, tsardom's political exiles and the hardiest of western explorers. In the whole western community of China there were then but two Britons who had made the journey there overland, largely by river-boat, dog-sleigh, camel and mule. At the 1900 exhibition in Paris visitors were provided with a simulated experience of what it was like to cross into the depths of Asia by *train de luxe*. Nagelmackers had commissioned two scenic artists from the Paris Opéra to traverse the route, recording their impressions on a vast stretch of canvas. In the Tuileries, for five francs a seat, people ate dinner on board one

of the Trans-Siberian's two restaurant cars – one decorated in the style of Louis XVI, the other in that of the *fin de siècle* – and watched through the windows as the scenic canvas unrolled, seemingly carrying them through Samara, Omsk, Tomsk, Irkutsk into Manchuria.

It was to those who saw it a startling preview of the world's first – and in the event the only – major intercontinental train service. And when it was inaugurated in reality some months later, the Russians felt a still greater sense of triumph than Nagelmackers himself. For a decade or more they had been ridiculed in the west for undertaking the Trans-Siberian project at all – it was almost universally accepted that it would be a white elephant of railways; for thinking that they could carry it out by themselves – the ineptitude of the Russians in practical matters was renowned; and indeed for carrying it out in such a chaotic fashion.

ABOVE LEFT One of the salons of the Trans-Siberian in 1900, complete with piano against the far wall.

LEFT A bridge across the Irtyche River on the Trans-Siberian. Many Western travellers expressed grave doubts about the safety of the Russian civil engineering works.

From Europe to Asia by Train de Luxe

RIGHT An early advertisement for the Trans-Siberian. The Tsarevitch attempted to sell tickets to Westerners before the line was completed, but this particular train never went into service, owing to lack of would-be passengers.

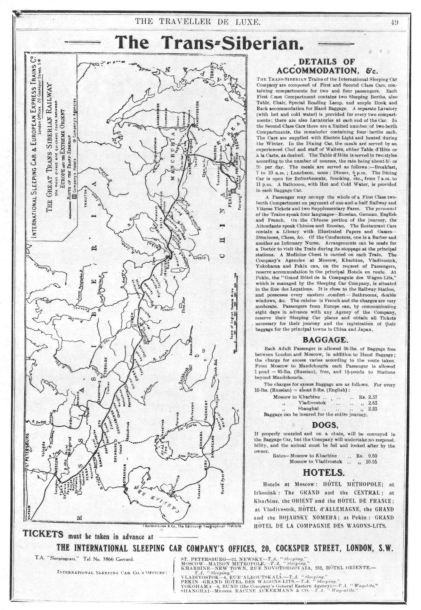

LEFT Details of the Trans-Siberian journey, 1909, showing the route from Warsaw to Vladivostok.

ABOVE The cover of a guide to the Trans-Siberian, 1903.

RIGHT A timetable for services from Central Europe to China. It took two weeks to travel overland to Peking.

Days				Time	Station	Time	Days			
Mo.	Tu.	Fr.	Sa.	1813	dep.Berlin (Schles.) p. 90 .... arr.	1023	Tu.	We.	Fr.	Sa.
Tu.	We.	Sa.	Su.	8 55	lep. Warsaw (Gl) p. 99A .... arr.	2134	Mo.	Tu.	Th.	Fr.
,,	,,	,,	,,	1740	dep. Stolpce c .... dep.	1322	,,	,,	,,	,,
,,	,,	,,	,,	2140	'ep. Niegoreloje ¶ .... arr.	1249	,,	,,	,,	,,
We.	Th.	Su.	Mo.	1135	arr. Moscow (Smolenski) ....dep.	2245	Su.	Mo.	We.	Th.
,,	,,	,,	,,	1619	d p Moscow (Smolenski) .... arr.	1832	,,	,,	,,	,,
,,	,,	,,	,,	1710	arr. Moscow (Severnii) ...... dep.	1735	,,	,,	,,	,,
We.	Tn.	Su.	Mo.	1745	dep. Moscow (Severnii) .... arr.	17 0	Su.	Mo.	We.	Th.
Th.	Fr.	Mo.	Tu	13 4	dep Viatka .... arr	2114	Sa.	Su.	Tu.	We.
Fr.	Sa.	Tu.	We.	8 22	dep Sverdlovsk ....dep.	2 31	,,	,,	,,	,,
Sa.	Su.	We.	Th.	3 42	arr. Omsk ... . dep	6 35	Fr.	Sa.	Mo.	Tu.
Sa.	Su.	We.	Th.	4 2	dep.Omsk .... arr.	6 15	Fr.	Sa.	Mo.	Tu.
				1626	lep.Novosibirsk .... dep.	18 7	Th.	Fr.	Su.	Mo.
Su.	Mo.	Th.	Fr.	9 44	lep.Krasnoyarsk .... dep.	I 8	,,	,,	,,	,,
				1537	lep.Kansk .... dep	1856	We.	Th.	Sa.	Su.
Mo.	Tu.	Fr.	Sa.	1222	arr. Irkutsk .... dep	2229	Tu.	We.	Fr.	Sa.
				13 2	lep.Irkutsk .... arr.	2147	,,	,,	,,	,,
Tu.	We.	Sa.	Su.	1530	arr. Karymskaya .... dep	2013	Mo.	Tu.	Th.	Fr.
Tu.			Su.	1532	lep.Karymskaya .... arr.	2010		Tu.		Fr.
Fr.			We.	3 19	arr. } Chabarovsk { dep	7 44		Su.		We.
,,			,,	3 44	dep. } { arr	7 19		,,		,,
Sa.			Th.	6 3	arr. Vladivostock‡ .... dep.	1837		Sa.		Tu.
—	We.	Sa.	—	1532	lep.Karymskaya .... arr.	2010	Mo.	—	Th.	—
—	Th.	Su.	—	3 20	arr. Manchouli ¶ .... dep.	8 10	,,	—	,,	—
—	Th.	Su.	—	1610	lep.Manchouli * .... arr.	7 10	Mo.	—	Th.	—
—	Fr.	Mo.	—	1330	arr. Harbin* .... dep	8 30	Su.		We.	
Daily				9 30	lep Harbin*.. .... arr.	1410	Daily			
				1525	arr. Hsinking* .... dep.	8 30				
				1630	dp (Changchun) .... arr.	7 0				
				2230	arr. Mukden* .... dep.	2340				
Cho. Ma. Exp.		Daily		2245	dep.Mukden .... arr.	2325	Daily.			
				7 40	arr. Dairen (Dalny) ...... dep.	1620				

CONNECTIONS
BERLIN—MOSCOW via Daugavpils.

			Time	Station	Time			
Mon.	Tue.	Fri.	2356	dep.Berlin (Schles.) p. 90A .. arr.	7 8	Tue.	Fri.	Sat.
			20 5	dep Daugavpils c .... dep.	1318	Mon.	Thu.	Fri.
Tue.	Wed.	Sat.	2145	dep Indra c .... dep.	1139	,,	,,	,,
			0 45	dep.Bigosovo .... dep.	1038	,,	,,	,,
Wed.	Thu.	Sun.	1555	arr. Moscow (Smolenski) .. dep.	19 5	Sun.	Wed.	Thu.

HARBIN—POGRANICHNAYA—VLADIVOSTOCK.

			Time	Station	Time			
Tue.	Thur.	Sat	7 30	dep.Harbin* .... arr.	16 0	Tues.	Thu.	Sun.
Wed.	Fri.	Sun.	1645	arr. Pogranichnaya* ....dep	6 15	Mon.	Wed.	Sat.
				dep.Pogranichnaya* .... arr.				
				arr. Vladivostock‡ .... dep				

MUKDEN—TIENTSIN—PEIPING.

		Time	Station	Time		
	1st day	2255	lep.Mukden .... arr.	6 35	2nd day	
	2nd day	1045	arr. Shanhaikuan .... dep.	1840	1st day	
Daily.	,,	195	arr. Tientsin (East) ....dep	1150	,,	Daily
	,,	20 0	lep.Tientsin ,, ...arr	1136	,,	
	,,	2317	arr. Peiping (Pekin) ...... dep.	8 45	,,	

MUKDEN—KEIJO—FUSAN—JAPAN.

		Time	Station	Time	
	1st day	23 0	dep.Mukden .... arr	2250	3rd day
Chosen	2nd ,,	2125	arr. Seoul .... dep.	7 0	,, ,,
Manchuria	3rd ,,	8 30	arr. Fusan .... dep	1955	2nd ,,
Express.	4th ,,	1655	arr. Tokio .... dep.	13 0	1st ,,

TIENTSIN—PUKOW—NANKING—SHANGHAI.

	Time	Station	Time	
1st day	1820	dep.Tientsin (East) .... arr.	7 10	3rd day
2nd ,,	2045	arr. Pukow .... dep.	I 40	2nd ,,
,,	2335	arr. Nanking .... dep	2315	1st day
3rd day	0 0	dep.Nanking .... arr.	2255	,,
,,	7 45	arr. Shanghai .... dep.	16 5	,,

Steamer services from Vladivostock to Japan, see page 306, and from Dairen to China and Japan, p. 308/310. TIME Moscow time is two hours later than that of Greenwich. When it is 12.0 noon at Moscow, it is 16.56 at Irkutsk, 18.0 at Harbin. Times at intermediate stations on the Trans-Siberian Railway are given in Moscow time. ¶ Moscow time ‡ Vladivostock time: 7 hours fast of Moscow time. * Manchukuo time: 6 hours fast of Moscow time. a Mid-European time. From Niegoreloje to Moscow, and from Moscow to Manchuria and Vladivostock (via Chabarovsk,) Sleeping Cars of direct communication, soft and hard class cars.

The derision had plenty of substance to it. The project was without question more of an indulgence in chauvinistic showing off than a practically based pursuit. Holy Russia, belonging neither to the industrialized west nor to the exotic east, and understanding neither, seemed to imagine that the building of the railway would somehow miraculously make it a major power in both. As it was primarily an exercise in chauvinism, foreign experts were rigorously excluded from even the smallest participation in the project from the outset through to its completion. The Russians lacked the human resources to carry it through competently by themselves, and the results of their attempting to do so were deplorable (and faithfully recorded in the railway journals of the west, whose editors appear to have viewed the prospect of the project's failure with relish). The surveyors went about their work in a breathtakingly slipshod

fashion. Working in the depths of winter, they plotted the route across frozen land without thought of the fact that for much of the year it would be a quagmire, incapable of supporting the weight of a train. They planned curves so tight that a train would be derailed going round them at a mere ten miles an hour. They were also corrupt, attempting to extort from each town they visited a fat bribe to plot the course of the railway through it. The elders of Omsk refused to pay up, on the seemingly irrefutable grounds that their city was the only important one in Siberia, so the surveyors could never hope to bypass it without their plan's being countermanded by their superiors in St Petersburg. The surveyors did bypass it, and their deliberate aberration was not noticed in the capital until the railway was complete, necessitating the costly construction of a loop line later.

Track-laying on the Central Siberian Railway in 1899. Owing to the unscrupulousness of surveyors and contractors alike, the work was carried out in breathtakingly slipshod fashion.

From Europe to Asia by Train de Luxe

If the surveyors lined their pockets through extortion, the contractors appointed to build the line were no more scrupulous. Paid according to the number of miles of track they laid each day, they considered it none of their affair that some of it (shades of Colonel Mann and his New Orleans, Mobile and Chattanooga Railroad) sank into the swamplands almost as soon as it was put down. The rails were made of the lowest grade of iron, and these were less than half the minimum weight and thickness of American ones. They snapped easily and often. Sleepers were green, uncured logs that warped and cracked as soon as the spring came. Bridges were constructed in such a rickety fashion that cars had to be rolled over them one by one, as they could not bear the weight of a train. The banks of cuttings were inadequately secured, and landslides were commonplace. Some were so much narrower than the minimum width stipulated from St Petersburg that coaches crashed into them, as they rocked from side to side at twenty miles an hour.

Added to the unscrupulous cupidity of the contractors was the fact that much of the labour force was made up of political prisoners, who hardly threw themselves enthusiastically into a project designed to be to the greater glory of the Tsar. Even had they wished to do so, they were too undernourished and otherwise ill treated to work effectively.

To reach the Pacific by the most direct route, the line had to be taken through the Chinese province of Manchuria, and the concession was duly purchased from the authorities. Chinese guards were recruited and armed with artillery to protect the line and its constructors from attack by brigand gangs. Then

A view through the Alexander II Bridge, which carried the Trans-Siberian over the Volga. The Russian railway administration was accused of devoting too much of its energies to embellishments and not enough to sound construction.

the uprising of the Society of Harmonious Fists – the 'Boxer Rebellion' – broke out. The guards turned their artillery on to the railway and blew it to pieces.

Eventually, however, the line was all but complete. The only gap was along the shores of Lake Baikal, which was to be crossed in a special ice-breaking ferry imported from Scotland. Trains began running between Europe and Asia and the first western travellers ventured forth to ride on them. Here are some extracts from the diary of one of the first Englishmen to go by rail from London to Shanghai; the journey took him eighteen days and seven hours, and cost him a total of £69 19s 7d in 1902:

'October 21: at 10 p.m. I left the hotel [in Moscow] in pouring rain and drove to the station where I was soon on board the Trans-Siberian Express, which started at 11 p.m. . . . I was about to go where but comparatively few Englishmen have ever been, and to pass through a region chiefly known to the civilized world as a place of exile, a place of horror, a dreary wilderness of frost and snow and wind, a place to which the words 'Ye who enter here, leave all hope behind,' were ever applicable. The greater part of this journey of over 5,000 miles from Moscow to the Far East, which I was about to make in a few days in a

The opening, in 1896, of the railway between the Black Sea and the Caspian Sea.

The train ferry which carried passengers across the Baikal. The ice breaker moored alongside the ferry was built in Scotland and dismantled for shipment to Siberia, where Russian engineers made several unsuccessful attempts to put it together before calling on Scottish aid. From the scrapbook of an Englishman, William Gray, who made the journey in 1908.

train de luxe, was, until recently, made by wretched exiles on foot, taking from one to two years.

'October 22nd: Passed through flat, uninteresting country. Much wheat cultivated. No trees, no hedges, no ditches, but little grass. Cloudy and depressing. Inhabitants ill-clad and poverty-stricken. Miserable houses with mud or wooden walls and thatch roofs.... Churches were the only substantial buildings.

'October 23rd: Same kind of country as yesterday.... Dining car too small and often have to wait hours for meals. General Wogack, a prominent Russian Officer on his way to the Far East, seeing that I could not get a seat, very kindly invited me to sit at his table, which had been reserved for him and his *aide-de-camp*. Both the General and his aide spoke English perfectly.

'Another passenger was a Chinese Secretary of Legation from Rome, who, not being able to speak anything but his own language, hailed me with delight, and we had long conversation in Mandarin.

172

'October 24th: This morning we were in the Ural Mountains, and at about ten o'clock stopped at Zlataoust, which is the last town in Europe, and where I bought two platinum candlesticks and a small model of a sledge as mementoes. Here also much cutlery was for sale at very low prices, being evidently manufactured in the neighbourhood, while precious stones were offered in the rough state, as taken from the mines, but it was necessary to be a connoisseur before venturing to buy. At Miasse, the next stopping place and the first station in Asia, saw many natives clad in skins with very yellow and Asiatic faces, dirty. Here I bought two crystal eggs as paper-weights. In a booth at one end of the platform, saw several stuffed specimens of game found in this neighbourhood. Wapiti, lynx, deer, wolf, fox, etc. Highest point reached by railway about 3,000 feet. Many nice views. Ground covered with snow, country very thinly populated.

'October 26th: This morning passed Obi, a town of considerable importance. The air was delicious. Snow on ground, with hard frost. Sun bright and warm. Country much nicer – more undulating. Saw men carrying stones for building purposes on a kind of tray with two handles at each end, as fishermen carry nets. China ponies were numerous here. Women and men were ugly and dirty. Sledges in use for carrying litter, hay, wood etc. To many stations, the most delicious milk and cream I have ever tasted were brought in bottles by women and girls for sale to passengers, and at very cheap rates. Occasionally, also, a few pears and apples of fair quality could be purchased, but the amount of fruit grown seemed to be small.

'October 27th: Much warmer, there being a good deal of snow, with bright sun. At about 2 o'clock reached Krasnoiarsk, a considerable town. Shortly after this crossed the river Yenesei on a magnificent iron bridge of several spans. The scenery became very fine in the afternoon, with pleasant hills and trees all covered with snow. Several China ponies in droves, sledges. . . . Saw many houses built underground with roof and entrance just appearing above snow.

'October 28th: Passing up a valley between lofty hills, noticed a corduroy road made of transverse trunks of trees. . . . At various points en route have seen the old Siberian Road of bitter memories.

'October 29th: Lovely morning with sharp frost. . . . Saw three small boys clad in furs fishing through a hole made in the snow-covered ice. At 11 o'clock reached Irkutsk but saw very little of it as the station is two miles out of town. At about 2 o'clock arrived at Lake Baikal, where we left the train and boarded the ferryboat "Baikal", a remarkable craft with four funnels and twenty windsails, three screws aft and one forrard. It was said that she could plough her way through ice two feet deep at eight miles an hour. I judged her to be about 260 feet

The Trans-Siberian
Express at Irkutsk
Station, 1908.

long and 50 wide. She has a good saloon where refreshments of all kinds can be obtained. . . . She has three lines of metals in the hold, so that three trains, each of about 240 feet long, can stand abreast. There were twenty or twenty-one trucks aboard today, but no engines. Most of the trucks were laden with railway metals. . . .

'No ice on lake. We cast off at a quarter to three in the afternoon and reach Missovaia on the other side at 5.35, a distance of only 40 miles, this being the narrowest part of the lake, the length of which exceeds 500 miles.

'The water was clear and of a steel-gray colour. Hills of perhaps 2,000 feet lined either shore as far as the eye could reach. Presently, the setting sun lit up the snow on the mountains with every colour of the rainbow, and we steamed along, as it were, between walls of flaming brilliancy. . . .

'At Missovaia we found another *train de luxe* awaiting us, and it was here, from the warmth of a saloon car, that I first saw a batch of Siberian exiles, although I had previously seen the cars with caged windows wherein they are now transported, instead of having to undergo that weary tramp of 4000 miles.

'It was already dark and the train had not yet started, when I saw a band of armed soldiers surrounding some thirty people carrying bundles, coming along the dimly-lighted platform, and then form up at one end of it, the people always being surrounded by the soldiers. What had especially attracted my attention, or I might not have noticed in the uncertain light of what the band consisted, was a little boy of about ten or twelve years of age, who was carrying a large bundle of what looked like clothing, trying to pass on the wrong side of some palings, when he was roughly seized by the ear by one of the Cossack guards and quickly brought back.

'Wishing to post some letters, I tried to pass along that end of the platform in search of the pillar-box, but was at once stopped by the guard. The steam from our engine, congealed by the sharp frost, fell in a fine snow about this luckless band, and glistened white on their clothes in the station lights, and it almost seemed to add an uncalled-for insult to the misery of their lot. I could not help wondering as to what their thoughts might be as they watched our waiting train replete with every comfort and blazing with electric light. I have never before seen the extremes of misery and captivity on the one hand, the extremes of freedom and luxury on the other, brought into such close and striking contrast, and I hope never to see it again. Subsequently, the dejected-looking throng, in which I fancied I saw women, were marched through a doorway into a darkened passage in the station, and so disappeared from sight.

'Probably they were all criminals who deserved their fate. Possibly not. Preconceived ideas and old tradition, however, stirred one's sympathies and left an unpleasant feeling in the mind for some time. I was constrained to compare our lots, and be thankful for mine. I, free to go my way in comfort. They . . .?

'October 30th: Another beautiful day. In the morning, we passed Petrovski zavod, a place historical in Russian annals as being the penal settlement of the conspirators who early in the nineteenth century tried to overthrow the ruling dynasty, and where numbers of the Russian aristocracy died in exile. It is now a large village of log houses, with wide, mud streets. . . . A large, black Russian cross, conspicuous on the highest peak of the surrounding hills, marks the burial spot of one of the most noble exiles. . . .

'In the afternoon, at Khilok station, we were stopped for a few minutes, I got out and ran up and down for exercise, but found the cold so great that I was glad to get on board again, for fear of having my ears frost-bitten, they having becoming perfectly numb.

'Since leaving Irkutsk, the houses have been better built, and the country has looked far more pleasing than in European Russia. I saw great piles of sleepers stacked alongside the line, and heavy metals lying by the tracks for many miles, so that the present light rails are apparently to be replaced, but so far, very few men at work. Today, we passed a wagon-church at a siding in a small village. The wagon-church moves up and down the line to places where there are no churches, and there it is stopped, and Mass said for the inhabitants by a Russian priest.

'A few fat-tailed sheep were also seen. These animals have enormous tails of solid fat, about as large, and of much the same shape, as a small ham. During the winter, when the frozen ground is covered with snow and no pasturage is to be found, it is said that they live on the fat stored in these tails, in the same manner as camels exist for considerable periods on their humps, seals on their blubber and bears by sucking their paws. . . .

From Europe to Asia by Train de Luxe

'Between Lake Baikal and Manchuria, all food was much dearer, while only American beer could be obtained and that at the exorbitant price of one rouble and a quarter, say half-a-crown, the bottle, which was because of excessive import duty. ... The Buriat population of this region looked of a low type, fairly large in stature but hideous and generally badly marked by smallpox. Saw one boy on skates. Bought postage stamps for 40 kopeks at a small station, but had to give another ten kopeks as commission. Saw a Mongol with a pigtail at one of the stations, which showed that we were approaching the borders of the Chinese Empire.

'October 31: Descended mountains at a good pace, having two engines, one in front and one behind. Were now in the country of the nomad Bactrians. No cultivation. Saw mobs of ponies and flocks of black and white sheep, cattle much resembling Scotch breeds, having long, thick hair, and a good

ABOVE The station at Tsvetko, 1896, typical of Siberian railway stations.

LEFT Tea-sellers at a Siberian country station. Their unappetising wares were offered at exorbitant prices.

BELOW A Russian postcard showing the Siberian-Manchurian frontier in 1908.

many two-humped camels. Observed one man shooting with a gun, another riding with bow and arrows slung on his back. The houses or wigwams were square in shape with arching roofs, and looked to be constructed of wickerwork and skins. In many places, noted irregular, flat stones set up on edge and varying in height from three to six feet, forming circles about twenty feet in diameter, in which, presumably, were graves.

'At Buriatskaia, which means capital of the Buriats, were two typical Mongols with pigtails and clad in skins. One of them was wearing an official tassel attached to his skin hood, but no official button to show his rank. Today saw a flock of larks, a hawk and a magpie. From daylight to dusk, during which time we travelled a distance of perhaps 300 miles, there was no vestige of either trees, shrubs, banks or hedges, and no cultivation, only the rolling grassland slightly whitened with snow. Reached the town of Manchuria, which is on the Manchurian frontier, at 8 p.m., and changed one of the first-class cars, something having gone wrong with the axles.

'November 1st: Saw many Mongols and Chinese. The country was hilly and sparsely wooded with silver birch and bushes. At Irekte the Russians have quite a colony. From Irekte to Boukhedou, a distance of about twenty-five miles, the line passes over some very steep hills. Two engines to haul us up, and coming down the descent was made in gradients, the train first running a mile or so one way, then stopping, when the engines were shunted to the other end, when we ran about a mile in the opposite direction, and so on, so that we described a perfect zigzag. . . . Boukhedou is already quite a large place with numbers of substantial Russian houses built of wood, and many more, as well as a station, in the course of completion. Sentries armed with rifles and revolvers were stationed every here and there along the line. Saw several long-haired goats, also some Chinese pedlars.

'November 2nd: We arrived at Harbin towards noon. I could see tall factory chimneys for some time previously, and then we crossed by a flat iron bridge over the Sungari river, whereon I saw about a dozen steamers laid up for the winter and a score or so barges.

'This large town, which has entirely sprung up since the advent of the railway, looked almost wholly Russian, there being a population of about 64,000 Russians and not so many Chinese. Russians here were even working as labourers, drivers of droskies etc. Many European houses and several large brick-built factories in the course of construction. The Russians are here with the intention of staying, and they are making good their hold as quickly as possible.

'The station is perhaps a mile from the river and of considerable size, though still in a rough stage. . . .

'After leaving Harbin, armed guards all along the line were

more numerous, while every few miles were brick-built block-houses surrounded by loop-holed walls. The country looked fertile and well cultivated, and the Manchu and Chinese inhabitants more prosperous. . . .

'November 3rd: Bright and warm. No trace of snow. At Tienline saw some rickshaws, also good, brick European houses being built. Chinese navvies working on the line, a good deal of rolling-stock and truckloads of superior-looking bricks. Chinese were *wheeling* barrow-loads of mud instead of, as is usual, carrying it in baskets, owing probably to the Muscovite persuasion. Country looked rich, well cultivated and well peopled, the women, being nearly all Manchus, having large feet. Chinese carpenters, bricklayers and joiners at work on many new stations.'

Through Mukden, the Manchurian capital, he passed to Dalny, seeing

'. . . many and substantial traces of Russian occupation [and passing] a mud fort, crowned with guns.

'For the whole journey the food on the train was good, but owing to the large number of passengers, after giving the order one sometimes had to wait from an hour to an hour and a half before getting served. After Baikal, this considerably improved, there then being two restaurants, one for smokers and one for non-smokers, whereas before, men smoked without restraint while women and children were eating their meals. This dining car was a perfect babble of tongues, for there were collected Russians, English, French, Japanese, Germans, Swiss, Chinese and Italians, generally all talking at once.

'On the whole, we rubbed along fairly well, although where so many nationalities were closely packed together for a fortnight, a certain amount of racial antipathy was bound to appear. When no Russians were about both the Japanese and Chinese would eagerly question me about the chances of war. When a Russian appeared, they immediately seemed to lose all interest in the subject. The Germans affected to despise the Russians, and the Russians said they hated the Germans, while they both respected the English.

'November 4th: We reached Dalny at 7 a.m., and I drove in a droski from the station to the wharves, a distance of perhaps one mile and a half, and there went on board the Rail Company's steamer *Amur* which was to convey us to Shanghai. It is truly wonderful to what a large European town Dalny has grown from absolutely nothing, in about five years. Good private residences, factories, hotels, shops, public buildings, the beginnings of botanical and zoological gardens, a dry dock . . . everything except the one thing needful: trade. Of the half dozen fine steamers in port, and others arriving or preparing to depart, all were practically light. Money has been poured out like water by the Russians in constructing the railway and building Dalny, and it is very doubtful if gigantic enterprise will ever be

made to pay. ... The Railway Company's line of superb steamers carrying mails, passengers and a little cargo between Dalny and Shanghai, is being run at a heavy loss.

'The impression left on me by my journey through Siberia is that Russia has advanced her outposts into Manchuria far beyond effective range of communication; that is communication by the Siberian railway alone, which is only a single line of light metals some 5,375 miles in length.

'Travelling over this line day and night for fourteen consecutive days, passing continuously through bleak, barren and almost unpopulated regions, crossing numerous wide rivers, an enormous lake and several mountain ranges, waiting sometimes for hours in sidings to allow homeward bound trains to pass, and seeing enough snow, even before winter had actually begun, to understand what difficulties heavy falls must occasion, I cannot help feeling that Russia's position in the Far East is unnatural and even precarious.

'The railway in its entirety is flimsy and liable to collapse almost everywhere, and I am certain it could never sustain a large volume of heavy traffic. ...

'The S.S. *Amur* cast off from her wharf at noon on November 4th, and after a quick and calm passage, arrived in Shanghai at noon on November 6th.'

Europe and the Far East had been linked, overland, for the first time. Nagelmackers published a timetable from London to Ostend, Brussels, Berlin, Warsaw, Moscow, Samara, Omsk, Irkutsk, Harbin, Changchung (change for Mukden and Peking) and Vladivostok. Thus it was possible to travel from Victoria Station in London to the extremity of the Orient with but three changes of train.

Another early passenger on the route was Harry de Windt, who had made the journey from Peking to Calais overland, some

A Russian Orthodox service on the Manchurian Railway, 1906, conducted from a specially built church on wheels. The Tsarevitch was more punctilious in providing railway employees with religious comforts than physical ones.

years earlier, before the railway was built, going much of the way by sleigh. The train, he said,

'. . . was truly an ambulant palace of luxury. An excellent restaurant, a library, pianos, bath, and last, but not least, a spacious and well-furnished apartment with every comfort, electric and otherwise (and without fellow-travellers) rendered this first "étape" of our great land journey one to recall with longing regret.

'We had nearly a fortnight of pleasant travel before us and resolved to make the most of it. Fortunately, the train was not crowded. Some cavalry officers bound for Manchuria, three or four Siberian merchants and their families, and a few Tartars of the better class. The officers were capital fellows, full of life and gaiety (Russian officers generally are), the merchants and their womenfolk sociable and musically inclined. Nearly everyone spoke French, and the time passed pleasantly enough, for although the days were terribly monotonous, evenings enlivened by music and cards, followed by cheery little suppers towards the small hours, almost atoned for their hours of boredom.

'Nonetheless, I cannot recommend this railway journey to those on pleasure bent, for the Trans-Siberian is no tourist line, notwithstanding the alluring advertisements which periodically appear during the holiday season. Climatically, the journey is a delightful one in winter, for Siberia is then at its best – not the Siberia of the English dramatist: howling blizzards, chained convicts, wolves and the knout, but a smiling land of promise and plenty even under its limitless mantle of snow. The landscape is dreary, of course, but most days you have the blue cloudless sky and the dazzling sunshine, so often sought in vain on the Riviera. At midday, your sunlit compartment is often too warm to be pleasant, when outside it is ten degrees below zero. But the air is too dry and bracing for discomfort, although the pleasant breeze we are enjoying here will presently be torturing unhappy mortals in London in the shape of a boisterous and biting east wind. On the other hand, the monotony after a time becomes almost unbearable. All day long the eye rests vacantly on a dreary white plain, alternating with green belts of wood-land, while occasionally the train plunges into dense, dark pine forest only to emerge again upon the same eternal "plateau" of snow. Now and again we pass a village, a brown blur on the limitless white, rarely a town, a few wooden houses clustering round a green dome and gilt crosses, but it is all very mournful and depressing, especially to one fresh from Europe.

'This train has one advantage. There is no rattle or roar about it as it steals like a silent ghost across the desolate steppes. As a cure for insomnia, it would be invaluable, and we therefore sleep a good deal and most of the day is passed in the restaurant. Here the military element is generally engrossed in an intermin-able game of *Vint* (during the process of which a Jewish civilian is mercilessly rooked) but our piano is a godsend and most Russian women are born musicians. So after *déjeuner* we join the fair sex who beguile the hours with Glinka and Tchaikovsky until they can play and sing no more. By the way, no one even knows the time of day and no one particularly wants to. Petersburg time is kept throughout the journey and the result is obvious. We occasionally find ourselves lunching at breakfast time and dining when we should have supped, but who cares? Although bottled beer at 8 a.m. might have unpleasant results in any other clime.

'The Ural mountains (which are merely downs) are crossed. Here the stations are built with some attempt at coquetry, for the district teems with mineral wealth, and in summer is much frequented by fashionable pleasure-seekers and invalids, for there are baths and waters in the neighbourhood. One station reminds me of Bad-Homburg or Wiesbaden with its gay restaurant, flower stall and a little shop for the sale of trinkets in silver and malachite and the precious stones found in this region. But beyond the Urals, we are once more lost in the desolate plains across which the train crawls softly and silently at the rate of about ten miles an hour. I know of only one slower railway in the world, that from Jaffa to Jerusalem, where I have seen children leap on and off the cars steps of the train while in motion, and the driver alight without actually stopping the engine, to gather wild flowers. . . .'

An insight into the kind of passenger who crossed from Europe to Asia in the early years is given by Sir Walter Harris, a British consular official in the Far East. On his way back to England, arriving in Nanking from Shanghai, with which it had become connected by rail, he stayed at the station hotel:

'One rainy afternoon after lunch, I was sitting in the dreary drawing room of the hotel. In a chair near me by the fire was an elderly grey-haired Scots lady – a pleasant godly woman of no mean intelligence but a little lacking in humour and not very quick on the uptake. We had met casually the afternoon before and conversed on the one topic of the day – the state of China. At the further end of the room, a group of young American men, employed in selling automobiles or the petrol by which automobiles are persuaded to move, were playing at poker.

'Quite suddenly, another lady appeared on the scene, a beautiful, young, quite inadequately clad creature of apparently Russian origin, who in spite of the change in fashion wore skirts that were too short for her. Speaking in French, she hailed the young men, kissing her hand to them and announcing her return to Nanking. She was received with joyful shouts of welcome and after a hurried conversation carried on with all of them at the same time, she departed to engage a room. Returning a minute or two later, she again blew them kisses from her impossibly rosy lips and announced with a smile of welcome that

One of the six magnificent salons on the Trans-Siberian Express, 1900.

A country station on the Vostok-China Railway, from William Gray's scrapbook, 1908.

A Japanese-owned, 'American style' locomotive, which connected the Trans-Siberian with the Chinese coast.

her room number was sixteen – and again the vision of youth and beauty was gone.

'Very slowly my elderly lady friend laid down her book and asked me: "Can you tell me why that young lady informed those men that her room was number sixteen?" I hastened to reply China was still in a disturbed state, that false alarms were liable to occur at times, and that no doubt she thought it advisable – as no doubt it was – that the gentlemen staying in the hotel should know where she slept, so that in case of danger they could see that she was adequately protected. My companion said nothing at the moment, but rising a few minutes later to leave the room she turned to the noisy group of card players and in a pleasant and inviting voice said: "Gentlemen, my room is number eleven." '

Despite de Windt's warning that the Trans-Siberian did not make for a model tourist excursion, tourism flourished right up to the outbreak of the First World War. Maybe few pleasure-seekers undertook the journey across Russia and into China more than once, and perhaps their principal motive was to be able to say that they had done so. But there were many more travellers, beyond doubt, than there were people with business to do at the other end. Nagelmackers soon found it necessary, and indeed profitable, to open another of his Palace hotels in Peking. The Japanese, who now ran the eastern part of the railway, built a modest hotel in Dairen, only to find that 'as a result of the largely increased tourist traffic' it was necessary to construct something far more ambitious. The result was 'a marvel of symmetry and elegance, 74 feet high', its ground floor covering half an acre. Soon it was attracting over ten thousand visitors a year. Even a seaside resort was developed by the Japanese to satisfy the demands of the European visitors.

Tzu Hsi, the Dragon Empress, dining on her Imperial train. An illustration from *Imperial Incense* by Princess Der Ling. Her Majesty insisted that the railway officials accompany her so as to execute without delay one or all of them, were something to go amiss.

No account of the coming of the railway to the Far East would be complete without mention being made of one of the most remarkable journeys ever taken, that of the Empress Tzu Hsi to Mukden, as related by her first lady in waiting, Princess Der Ling.

The Russian royal family had gone quite a long way towards laying claim to having the outstanding royal train of the world – against strong competition from Queen Victoria and various German monarchs. According to one account, published in 1901, when the Tsar travelled on the Trans-Siberian, it was in what was

'. . . without doubt the costliest train in the world. In interior furnishings, it surpasses in magnificence the *train de luxe* lately built for the German Emperor. It is a palace on wheels. . . .

'The walls of the drawing room are covered with pale rose silk, while the Royal bedchamber is hung with light blue satin, the furniture being covered with cretonne of the same colour. Each of the sleeping salons has a bedchamber attached as well as a dining room, upholstered with chamois leather.

'When travelling the study, which is fitted for all conveniences of transacting business, is the principal room of the Tsar.

'There is in this train a carriage devoted to the children's playroom, while the nursery, with fair-like swinging cots, is nearby. Experts recommend the use of milk from the same cow, and hence the little daughters of the Tsar take their own cows with them when they travel. On a recent visit of the Tsar to Germany, a palatial cow car, with two Holstein cows, was attached to the Imperial train.

'The last carriage is for the train officials, and comprises a study, a sitting room, and several coupés, well stocked with apparatus, as the whole of the train is governed from here. Each carriage is in telephone communication with the others, while the systems of heating, ventilating and lighting are unsurpassed.'

Nobody knew then that Tzu Hsi's imperial yellow sixteen-coach royal train was more magnificent still, because no commoner – beyond its constructors – had ever seen it. Nor, for several years after its delivery, did the Dragon Empress herself see it – she had ordered it not so much with any thought of using it, but because other monarchs had one.

But she did eventually decide that she would visit her native Mukden, and do so by rail. Her ministers petitioned her against the project: 'Never before in Chinese history has a Sovereign made a journey by railway. It is very dangerous. Particularly it is dangerous to Her Majesty, who is becoming old. Nor can Her Majesty be spared so long from the Forbidden City where she has so many duties to perform. Her Majesty's humble servants beg that she will give over her plan, that she will not be swayed by alien influences.' Her Majesty tore the paper into tiny shreds and replied: 'What difference does it make that no other [Chinese] Sovereign has made a railway journey? Perhaps they would have had there been railways. We are not afraid of danger either. We face danger without fear. And what right have you to say that we are old?'

The preparations for the journey were daunting, partly because so many problems of court etiquette were posed by the new conveyance. Her Majesty had insisted that the drivers and firemen be eunuchs, and it took some time to persuade her that it was possible neither to castrate trained railway mechanics, nor to teach men accustomed to acting as valets and waiters how to drive a train safely, particularly in the time available.

She conceded the point, while still insisting that the rule be observed that no servant should seat himself in the same building – as the train was held to be – as herself. Therefore the engineers had to drive in an upright position, and to rest had to lie down completely (thus ensuring that they were at a lower level than her imperial feet). She also insisted that they should wear the court uniform of eunuchs as they stoked the furnace – 'Imagine', remarked Princess Der Ling, 'the fireman stoking a fire with dirty coal, dressed in a mandarin hat resembling nothing so much as a mushroom, wearing boots of black satin and a gown to rival the beauty of the rainbow. But so it was – Her Majesty's word was law on the matter.'

As the visit was to be a short one she took with her but forty pairs of shoes and two thousand gowns, which required a coach to themselves. So did the royal sedan chair, which she took with her to continue her journey should trains prove to be as unreliable a means of transport as their detractors had claimed. Two coaches were set aside as kitchens – in the one, the chopping of the food into small, intricately shaped pieces was done; in the other, the two walls were lined with stoves, each tended by a master cook and two assistants who specialized in the preparation of only two kinds of dish each. As it took so very long to prepare some of the dishes – dinner consisted of one hundred courses, only three or four of which the old tyrant actually ate – the kitchen was a place of constant activity.

The atmosphere on board the railway officials' coach was was one of fear. Her Majesty had insisted that they should accompany her on the train, so that if something did go amiss she could order the execution of one or all of them forthwith.

The throne room on the train was made to resemble that in her residence in the Forbidden City as closely as possible:

'The bedroom occupied the forward end of the car. The only furniture in it was the huge bed of polished teak. Above the wide bed was a teak canopy from which hung curtains of blue silk, embroidered with crab apple blossoms. These blossoms were used because the crab apple was an indication of spring. The only other article was the inevitable small stool, some three inches in height, of teak, upholstered with yellow silk, beside the bed. . . . Between the windows were Chinese paintings of the best painters, ancient and modern, and under the paintings were shelves on which various toilet articles were set. The windows were curtained with yellow silk.

'A partition separated the bedroom from the throne room, and the throne room was as luxurious as could be imagined. No expense had been spared to make it attractive, comfortable and in keeping with the best court traditions. Four porcelain pots, each containing flowers, rested on four stands in the corners of this room. . . . The rug or carpet which covered the entire floor of the throne room was of blue velvet, marked profusely with designs in gold, of the peony and the phoenix. The windows were widely spaced to allow room between them for shelves on which to place her Majesty's most treasured curios – the things at which she never tired of looking. The curtains were of plain yellow silk with gold tassels, and between the windows were other paintings of her favourite Chinese artists. These paintings were always of legendary happenings in Chinese history. The vases, or pots, which held the four flowers of spring, were very smooth and covered with landscape paintings in which were human figures out of the Middle Kingdom legendry. Besides the four pots were several small vases, set on stands built especially for them. In these vases, the Empress Dowager kept her favourite blossoms, in water, atop which the blossoms, stemless, floated. The result was beautiful and fragrant.

'The rest of the car contained two small rooms – one the room in which the court ladies rested when not on duty, and behind that the room in which Chang Teh – the table eunuch – and such other eunuchs as he might select for duty, kept water boiling over a charcoal stove, for the Empress Dowager's tea. She liked several brands – jasmine, lotus and other kinds which are unknown outside China, even now.

Another illustration from *Imperial Incense* showing the Empress descending from her train at Tientsin. Her journey to Mukden was strongly opposed by court officials, which increased her delight in undertaking it.

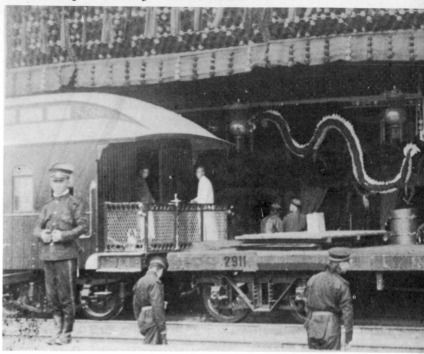

'Fastened to the forward part of the partition which separated the small compartment of the court ladies from the throne room, was a canopy, under which was Her Majesty's throne. The throne was smaller than those usually affected by her in the Forbidden City, but it was a beautiful thing. It was of polished ebony inlaid with jade. The seat was of yellow upholstery. Behind the chair was the inevitable screen. It was also of ebony, polished, and studded with jade and precious stones. The screen was an integral part of the throne. One was never used without the other, the practice dating back nobody knows how many centuries.

'Between the throne and the partition was a small day bed where Her Majesty could rest whenever it suited her to do so.

'I was with Her Majesty when she first entered her car to begin the trip. It took her a moment or two to get her bearings, for though the throne room resembled in every respect her other throne rooms – of which she had many – the dictates of space required that it should be much smaller, and she seemed to have difficulty in adapting herself to the change. But she soon managed it, instructing the eunuchs to make sure that her throne faced forward so that she could ride facing the engine. She gave a few instructions for the placing of her curios and gave orders for the train to start. She seemed very pleased with everything and, though she was then nearly seventy years of age, was like a child with a new toy. Here, in this transplanting of a palace, she showed her power. . . .

The Imperial train
standing in Peking
Station, decorated for
the occasion. When the
train set off, Princess
Der Ling was amazed to
find Her Majesty
'almost smiling' with the
excitement, perhaps for
the first time in many
years.

'Not the best engineer in the world could start even an
imperial train without some lurching motion. At least the one
we had could not. There we were, all standing, while Her
Majesty seated herself on the throne thoroughly to enjoy her
trip, when the train started. Her shelves were packed with all
manner of small ornaments – which immediately came tumbling
down. My heart sank into my very shoes. That an engineer would
dare to shake Her Majesty! I knew she would think of it that way.
And I, together with Chin San, had had much to do with the
arranging of things in this car, on the shelves – everything. And
here at the first motion of the train they all went clattering to the
floor. I could see someone getting beheaded and was none too
sure it would not be myself. . . .

'All dashed to the shelves trying to catch the falling objects,
to try to keep other things from falling. The court, for the
moment, was as undignified as could possibly be. I waited,
expecting some grim command from Her Majesty. I turned to
her afraid to look – to find her almost smiling, perhaps for the
first time for many years.'

The train was stopped. The ornaments were put back on the
shelves and secured, as were the porcelain flower pots, and the
royal progress to Mukden, at five miles an hour in the train of
imperial yellow, was under way.

10. Around the World in Fifty Days

The inauguration of the Canadian Pacific made it possible to go around the world travelling overland for two-thirds of the journey.

In the 1870s the fictitious Mr Phineas Fogg astounded the reading public by travelling round the world in eighty days. His creator, Jules Verne, did not trouble to go over the territory himself before writing about it, but worked out the journey from a Bradshaw timetable, while sitting in the village of Le Crotoy in Normandy.

Not many years later – indeed by the turn of the century – it was not only possible to confirm from Bradshaw that, thanks to international railway developments, it was possible to go round the world in fifty days, mostly overland, but people actually began to do so – though few of them had so little leisure that they had to make the journey in the shortest time possible.

Nagelmackers joined forces with the Canadian Pacific Railroad to ease their path; and the most popular route was from London to Liverpool, by CPR steamer to Montreal, by rail to Vancouver, by steamer again to Yokohama, by rail again to Nagasaki, by steamer again to Vladivostok, and thence via the Trans-Siberian to Moscow, and via the Nord Express back to London.

Of the sea voyages I shall say nothing. On the Canadian section of the journey, a privately published diary of the journey has come into my hands:

'SCENE: The Station of the Canadian Pacific Railway, Montreal, 20 o'clock.

'Cab no. 1 drives up and deposits an Anglican parson, carrying a walking stick, portmanteau and satchel – first on the ground – Dean Carmichael.

'Cab no. 2 drives up and deposits another Anglican parson, carrying light overcoat, portmanteau and sundry satchel – second on the ground – Canon Empson.

'Cab no. 3 drives up and deposits two lay gentlemen, Mr White, Manager of the Gazette Printing Co., and Mr Wm White, QC.

'It is plain, from the greetings, that these gentlemen meet by appointment, and equally plain that they constitute a party about to take the longest continuous railway trip that can be taken, namely, from Montreal on the St Lawrence, with its tides from the Atlantic, to Burrard Inlet, British Columbia, whose tides roll in from the Pacific; thence down the inlet by steamer to Victoria, capital of Vancouver Island – an island on whose further shore one can stand with the happy thought that nothing lies between him and Japan and China, save the deep blue seas.

'At the start of the journey, some formal business was transacted. Mr Richard White was unanimously appointed guide, Chancellor of the Exchequer and General Traffic Manager; Mr W.White QC was appointed Judge of the Supreme Court, in order to decide any problems of a legal character that might arise during the journey; Dean Carmichael was appointed secretary, taking notes of travel, which it was

RIGHT Four locomotives crossing the Stony Creek trestle in British Columbia.

BELOW An open-plan sleeping carriage in a Canadian Pacific train. Many around-the-world travellers took this route across North America.

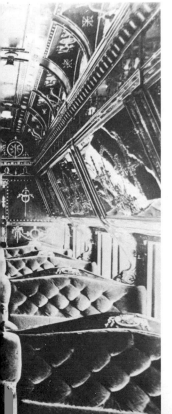

unanimously agreed should be printed, at the expense of the General Manager, for private distribution; and Canon Empson was appointed the friend and the companion of all concerned. It was also agreed that, as far as practicable, the party should keep together, on the distinct understanding that the utmost freedom should be allowed to all. After the transaction of the business, the Manager and the Judge disappeared into the smoking room at the end of the car, and the clerical members went to bed. . . .'

The Dean wrote of the history of the construction of the railroad, which need not detain us, before continuing to describe the carriages:

'As for the "Sleeping" or first-class cars, one has only to travel a straight stretch of three thousand miles in one of them to give a verdict – all along the line – in their favour. Each car is a luxuriously furnished drawing room, well ventilated and lighted, with large plate-glass windows giving a wide field of vision – with bathrooms, and washrooms, and smoking rooms, electric bells and hot-air heating apparatus, and in the night, each compartment changed into a sleeping room that one has only to get accustomed to, to rest in soundly. Lasting luxury, cool comfort, such in fine, is the SPR day car for first-class passengers.

'Then comes the commissariat. Enter porter vested as to his upper man in white. "Dinner ready." Rush out of drawing room car into dining-room on wheels; with waiters standing like soldiers, one to two tables, each table set as in private dining room. Bill of fare – soup, fish, entrees, vegetables, pastry, fruit, tea and coffee; sit as long as you like and pay three shillings stg. for as good a breakfast, dinner and tea as any reasonable man would ask to have laid before him.

'[Another] blessing of the CPR is punctuality. The day has past when express trains pulled up to allow officials to pick blackberries or to "liquor up" when travellers waited five or ten hours at leading stations, or built up fires in a box stove in the waiting room of way stations, or lay full-stretch on a form, with a portmanteau for a pillow. There are memories of the past

> Like the dew on the mountain
> Like the foam on the river

faithful Scotchmen may sing a Coronach over them

> Like the bubble on the fountain

as far as the CPR express trains are concerned

> They are gone, and forever.

'Thursday: Woke up to find the train passing by the side of the Ottawa river, through an uncultivated country. From North Bay, on Lake Nipissing, out, the country becomes rough and rocky and is studded with a number of beautiful lakes apparently running into one another. At Sudbury Junction come across Dr Wylde, who has charge of a section of the railway, looking strong and hearty. . . .

'Friday: Woke up on the shores of Lake Superior; air delightfully cool and morning beautiful. The scenery all along this section is charming, and sometimes strikingly grand, the rail following the coast very closely. The waters of the lake are of the bluest blue and near the shore are as clear as crystal. Glorious ground for the photographer and painter – the clear sky, the curving coastline, the blue water, the rich, salmon-coloured rocks rising from flats into mountains that rear their rounded heads to meet the brilliant sunlight. The curves and turns of the rail are wonderful, giving a ceaseless variety of scenery, with the lovely lake or inland ocean always present. . . .

'After tea the Canon and I sat out on the hind platform of the car and saw muskeg in every shape and form and depth of colouring, and the boats, left behind by Lord Wolseley in the Red River Expedition, rotting away the balance of their lives, no settlers near to break them up. The sun did not go down till a quarter to nine. There was a good deal of good-humoured chaffing as night came on about the berths. There was an invasion of the old settlers in the train at Port Arthur, and a number of ladies and children squatted on our sections. It did not matter much during the evening, but there was an unpleasant feeling among the original settlers as to whether the squatters would remain squatted during sleeping hours. However, it turned out that all the squatters had obtained upper berths, and then the lower-berth gentlemen were taught a lesson in the virtue of resignation. I had an upper berth all along (memo – always take an upper berth. It is cool and you can go to bed early and read) so I had to resign nothing, but our manager, Mr White, resigned with spontaneous gracefulness.

'The beds were not made up till 11 o'clock, and I was dead tired and so was the Canon.

'Saturday: . . . Arrived at Winnipeg sharp on time. The car was so full we found it hard to sort out our traps, and the Judge came off leaving his umbrella behind him. The station was a scene of wondrous bustle, and was crowded along the whole platform, which is a very large one. Everywhere one saw faces well known, and sometimes not seen for years. Archdeacon Fortin and his curate, the Rev. Joseph Merrick and Capt. W. Johnston were waiting for us. Fortin opened fire at once for three sermons on Sunday, Mr Merrick came to take us to his house and the Captain came to see that the faintest wish on our part would be carried out. After a very short delay – for our General Manager is a rusher – we drove up to the Clarendon, a fine-looking Hotel within sight of Fortin's church, which is well worthy of Montreal, or New York, so far as architectural beauty is concerned. The Canon and I got splendid rooms, the judge a very good one, but somehow our General Manager got very inferior quarters. Just as I was shutting my door, he darted past me right on the warpath for the landlord – a solemn-looking man not accustomed to being run round as he will be in a few moments when the General Manager gets on his trail. . . .

'Monday: . . . This is Dominion Day and every little village along the line has its celebrations. It gave us a good opportunity of seeing the settlers, for all crowded to the stations along the line, and after eyeing them over we came to the following conclusions: 1st, they were all young men and young women. 2nd, they were all sober. 3rd, they were all strong and healthy-looking and well dressed. 4th, they were in every way far ahead (if appearance be a sign of prosperity) of the men who originally settled the country. In fact, in rural Canada I never saw a more respectable-looking crowd, and the palpable absence of King Whiskey was singularly refreshing. . . .

'Tuesday: . . . We get out at the railway station at Maple Creek for a few minutes to take stock in the real live Indian men, women and children (Crees) that were scattered over the platform. The men were painted lavishly, vermilion and brick-coloured faces, toned down with blue and yellow streaks. The women were remarkable for brilliant blankets, and some of the girls had large slabs of mother-of-pearl hanging from their ears.

As far as the men and women were concerned, they might as
well have been inmates of the deaf and dumb asylum. . . . There
they sat, or leaned, against the station, or stood out on the
platform, straight as a Douglas pine, silent and quiet as clams.
Two splendid-looking fellows sat with their chins in their hands
and their eyes fixed on the brasswork of the engine glittering in
the sunlight, and never seemed to move once. I should not think
that the Crees would make good commercial travellers. Each
Indian had a pair of polished buffalo horns for sale, but they
never offered them to anyone; indeed, for the matter of that,
they appeared that it was perfectly immaterial to them whether
they sold them or not. If you thirsted for a buffalo horn, you
had to open up negotiations. "What do you charge for these?"
Up would go two or three Indian fingers, coupled with the word
"bits" implying two or three quarters. Then, if the bargain was
completed, the horns changed hands; but if not, the Indian
looked away out on the prairie, ignoring your existence, calmly
waiting some other claimant for his wares.

'Here also on the platform are members of the mounted

The first Canadian
Pacific passenger train
at Port Moody, 4 July
1886.

police, as soldier-like cavalrymen as you would find anywhere
in the British army. Major Antrobus – every inch a soldier –
boarded the cars here in company with his wife, and we had a
very pleasant chat with him between Maple Creek and Forres,
the next station, where he left the cars. . . .

'At 16 o'clock we reached Medicine Hat, situated on the
South Saskatchewan river, quite a pretty little village, with
about 100 houses in it, and two churches, one evidently Anglican.
The station platform was covered with Blood and Blackfeet
Indians, got up in paint and feathers, and in every way a more
jovial party than our friends the Crees. One strapping fellow
had a tame thrush roosting on his hat, and appeared to enjoy the
fun that this novel headgear produced. Another fellow was all
got up in the most gorgeous style – feathers and paint, bright
blanket, embroidered sleeves and leggings, dandy shells, and
such like. I felt like asking him: "Pray sir, are you anybody in
particular?" But on more private inquiry I was told that the
Indians, like the white men, had their "dudes" and that this
was the "boss dude" of Medicine Hat. All of them had buffalo

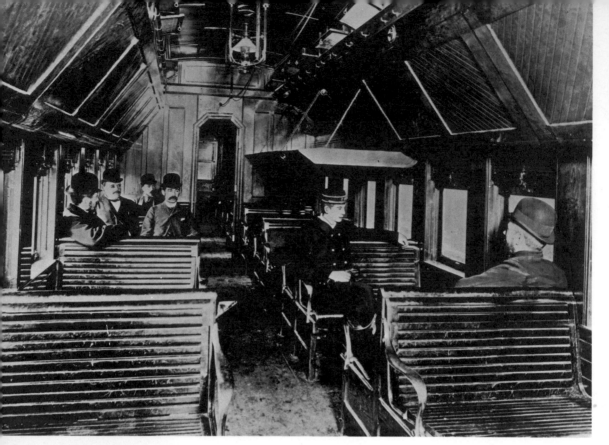

ABOVE An early type of sleeping car on the Canadian Pacific Railroad. Conditions improved later.

OPPOSITE Reconstruction of a nineteenth-century first class carriage of the Canadian Pacific Railroad.

OVERLEAF A Howard Stanton map of the Trans-Siberian Railway.

horns for sale, but, like the Crees, they never offered to sell, but waited calmly for negotiations to be opened by passengers. . . .

'All through today's journey, piled up at the leading stations along the road, were vast heaps of the bones of the earliest owners of the prairie – the buffalo. Giant heads and ribs and thigh bones, without one pick of meat on them, clean as a well-washed plate, white as driven snow, there they lay like a giant sacrifice on the altar of trade and civilisation. A leading and well-known Roman Catholic missionary told our Mr White (who picks up information everywhere and from everybody) that he often longed for the old days when buffalo marched in stately strides along its trail, and the Indian lived out his wild and natural life. One can easily realise the feeling; but surely one railway whistle – full of prophecy for Church, for State, for Indian, for white man – must in the long run atone one thousand fold for the loss of all that herds of buffalo implied. . . .

'Tonight we bid goodbye to the prairies, and the morning will find us in the Rockies. . . .

'Wednesday: This has been a whitestone day in our lives, for when we woke, at 4.50, we found ourselves right into the Rocky Mountains, drawing near to Banff. I had gone to bed very sleepy, and had slept like a top, and had tumbled out with but one idea on my mind, namely, that of being first in the washroom. The same idea, however, had long before struck the

196

STANFORD'S MAP OF
THE SIBERIAN RAILWAY
THE GREAT LAND ROUTE TO
CHINA AND KOREA

Canon and several other gentlemen; so, in that flannel-headed state of brain that getting up at 4.50 is apt to bring about, I went into the smoking room and looked in a stupid way out of the windows. I tell you, the stupidity left me in an instant, as one glance reminded me where I was. There they were, the most gigantic and roughest mountains I ever looked at, and so close to you that you felt instinctively as if you were within walls. Mountains like giant saws, like lonely castles, like hump-backed camels. . . .

'We arrived at Banff right on time, and were driven in an omnibus along a good road up to a palatial hotel, standing in a lofty elevation and belonging to the CPR. It was very cold driving up and the empty grate in the large hall seemed to make it colder, but after a good wash, and a hearty breakfast, we sat on the sunny side of the house, at an altitude of 4,500 feet, with the grandest view of mountain scenery we could ask to see, lying out at our feet, the valley of the Bow, hemmed in with its attendant mountains, a view that would repay a person for the whole journey. In the meantime, our ever-moving manager, Mr White, had hunted up Mr Stewart, the superintendent of the national park in which the hotel is situated, who kindly consented to show us round his territory. . . .'

They toured the park, drank from and bathed in the sulphur springs, and so back to the hotel, where

'. . . a bright log fire roared and crackled in the wide-mouthed grate, and we sat round it as the guests talked and chattered until one by one, the circle came less, the fire became low, our party making for bed with the prospect of an early start in the morning.

'Thursday: Up at 4.50 – coffee – left Banff 5.10, sharp on time.'

They went on up through the Rockies, made the slow descent again, entered the Fraser Canyon and were now approaching Vancouver.

'Friday: We breakfasted at North Bend at 7.30 and had a rich banquet of fruit, peaches, apricots, large purple plums and oranges. Leaving the Bend sharp on time we passed through a series of tunnels cut out of the rocks on the bare mountainside, the river running deep down beneath us. This whole section of the country is very beautiful, as the mountains are wooded in some cases from base to summit. All the workers you see along the line are Chinamen – men melancholy-faced, plaited hair, low, stunted-looking Chinamen – some of them the ugliest looking mortals I ever looked at, but, for men doing hard railway work, unusually clean-looking. At Yale, a village locked in glorious wooded mountains, we saw from the track a modest Joss House, just like any other frame house, except that it had vermilion coloured walls, all covered with Chinese characters, hung up on its front. . . .'

At lunchtime they reached Vancouver, and from thence

OPPOSITE The risqué reputation which the Orient Express swiftly acquired inspired a bawdy Parisian musical comedy, advertised in this poster.

OPPOSITE A wooden
bridge in the Rockies.

BELOW LEFT A Japanese
illustration of the
Shiodome Railway
building. Japanese
railways became a
tourist attraction in their
own right.

LEFT The first passenger
train to cross Canada
arrives in Vancouver
from Montreal, 1887.
Europeans flocked to
Canada to view the
countryside through the
window of a railway car.

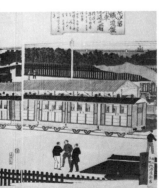

travelled to Victoria, where they went to the Driard House –
'the most comfortable hotel I ever stopped in. We had lofty and
well-ventilated rooms, admirable attendance in room and at
table, and the cookery would have done credit to the best-
managed club. After we had washed and rubbed off marks of
journeying, we started to see the sights by gaslight.'

Thus ended the second leg of a turn-of-the-century journey
round the world. The next stop was Yokohama.

Japan's economic success was already an international tourist
attraction; and here westerners paused on their way round the
world to wonder at a people who seemed to live in their homes
and socially as though they were still in the Middle Ages, and

A dining car on the Sanyo Railway, which opened in 1898. As an alternative to Western cuisine many foreigners ordered Japanese delicacies served in lacquer boxes.

yet ran advanced industrial enterprises. An exceptionally broad-minded, globe-trotting English vicar of the period, the Rev. Frank Thatchell, recommended also a visit in Tokyo

'. . . to the quarter where the members of the oldest profession in the world reside. . . . The Yoshiwara of Tokyo is entered by a single gate called *Omon*. There are six wide streets and many alleys. The girls sit behind bars in brilliantly lighted rooms open to the street and are not allowed to solicit passers-by. Notwithstanding the beauty of the dresses and the luxury of the rooms, these houses are only considered third class. The second-class houses show photographs of their inmates and the first-class ones have no display at all.'

He also counselled dismounting from the train between Yokohama and Nagasaki, to stay at a country inn:

'On arriving, you take off your boots and are conducted to what is to be your bedroom and living room. The maid who is allotted to you is called the *Nesan*, or Elder Sister, and she brings in a cushion for you to sit on, a charcoal fire box and finally tea. While drinking this you prepare the *chadai* or tea money, which takes the place of tips given on leaving the hotel in England. It should be wrapped in paper, or, better still in the little envelopes (*Kaneire*) which are sold in the shops for that purpose. The tip is divided into two portions, and one yen for the master and 50 sen for the *Nesan* is usually given for a stay of a few days.

'After drinking the tea, you leave the envelopes on the tray.

In a little while the maid comes in and carries off the tray, pretending not to notice the tea money, but, in a few minutes, the master and all his servants come in, rubbing their knees and drawing in their breath in token of respect, and thank you by touching their heads on the floor.'

The Rev. Thatchell advised that one should not be embarrassed if, while bathing, a girl came in to rub one's back:

'[After dinner] one night you may like to have a geisha to amuse you. . . . The fee is 25 sen the hour and one yen tip, and it is paid in the hotel bill.

'When you want to go to bed, clap your hands and tell the *Nesan*. The bed is kept in a cupboard in your room, and consists of several mattresses and a *kimono* in which you sleep. The pillow is packed tight with rice or tea, but if you have a small air cushion you will be comfortable enough. If tired, it is refreshing to have in a masseur. He is invariably a blind man and will gently knead your body in a traditional way, working always from the heart. The *Nesan* then brings you a night lamp, and takes out the firebox, as the fumes are dangerous, before bidding you goodnight. You will hear no further sound except the night watchman in the street, who beats two pieces of stick together as he goes along, to assure the householders of his watchfulness.'

Travelling across the country by train, visitors remarked how excellent the carriages were – fully up to American or European standards, with delicately inlaid wood panelling. Meals were a particular attraction, surpassed only by the civility and honesty of the railway servants.

'When your train stops in Japan [wrote an anonymous correspondent to the *Railway Herald* in 1901] they sell you what is called Bento – that is, a lunch. It is in a little two-storey box, the lower storey of which is filled with rice, while the upper storey has some fish or vegetables, and perhaps you might get a bit of chicken in there. There are two prices for those lunches. One is twelve sen, which would be six cents in the United States, and the other is twenty-five sen. I was new to the country and got these two prices mixed up. I ran after the coolie boy [selling lunches]; everybody was rushing after him. I chased him down four or five cars and got a box of Bento and asked him the price. I understood him to say it was twenty-five sen, and gave him twenty-five sen before rushing back to my compartment. I got in there, and I soon heard the sound of flying cogs running after me. There was the boy with thirteen sen in his hand, putting it in the car window. He had neglected his business and turned down a lot of people who wanted to buy lunch from him, in order to return that money to me which I had overpaid him. I think almost any American boy like that would have thought that the Lord had sent him that thirteen cents, and he ought to keep it.'

The tourists in Japan found themselves to be attractions:

ABOVE The first sleeping car on the Sanyo Railway. According to one account, Japanese ladies preferred sitting up all night to lying down and damaging their hairstyles.

OPPOSITE Advertisement for the Chosen Railway of Korea.

'When a Japanese coolie wants to look at a thing, he looks at it. He would flatten his nose right against the glass and look at you just as long as he wanted to. So when we stopped at a station at night, there would be a row of noses flattened against the glass all the way down the length of the train.

'The most amusing thing about the sleeping cars is the manner in which Japanese ladies travel in them. The Japanese lady has a habit of doing her hair up in a very artistic manner and quite a permanent way, fixing it so the air can blow through it; when that is done in the proper order and fastened she does not want to have it disturbed, so she sleeps on a device called a makura. On that she rests her neck; therefore she can turn back and forth as much as she likes during the night without disturbing her hair. But the makura and sleeping cars do not agree with one another at all. If the engineer takes up the slack of the train a little bit sharply, over goes the makura and twenty cents of hairdressing is gone. Consequently, when the gentlemen of that region travel with their wives on sleeping cars, they pay two yen for a berth for their ladies, who sit up in them all night.'

The shortest passage from Japan to the Asian mainland was to Fusan, in southern Korea, but twelve hours sea voyage away. From there it was a ten-hour train journey to Seoul, where the railway company ran an excellent hotel; and from there one

206

CHOSEN RAILWAY
KOREA

To TOKYO
via CHOSEN.

From Mukden	-	2½ days
,, Tientsin	,,	4 ,,
,, Peking	,,	
,, Changchun	,,	3 ,,
,, Harbin	,,	
,, Moscow	-	11 ,,
,, Berlin	-	13 ,,
,, Paris	,,	14 ,,
,, London	,,	

NATIVE PORTERS.

CHOSEN-MANCHURIA. EXPRESS.

Tri-weekly Service between Fusan and Changchun. Leaves Fusan every Sunday, Tuesday and Friday. Leaves Changchun every Monday, Wednesday and Friday. Excellently equipped 1st Class Sleeping, 2nd Class Sleeping, and Dining Cars attached. Connected with the Trans-Siberian Express.

DAILY EXPRESS SERVICES.
FUSAN-KEIJYO (SEOUL)-ANTUNG-MUKDEN.

Two Express Trains, having 1st, 2nd and 3rd and Dining Cars, are run twice a day from Fusan to Antung, and vice versa. One of these Trains takes 1st and 2nd Class Sleeping Cars on the Fusan-Keijyo (Seoul) Section, and the other runs conjointly with Trains on the Antung-Mukden Line, which connect with those to and from Changchun, Dairen, Peking, etc.

| FUSAN STATION HOTEL. | NANDAIMON REFRESHMENT ROOM. |
| SHINGISHU STATION HOTEL. | DINING CAR SERVICE. |

Under the direct Management of the Railway.

Good Accommodation. ∴ Best Attendance. ∴ Moderate Charges.

For particulars please apply to the Bureau.

EXPRESS LEAVING FUSAN PIER.

RAILWAY BRIDGE OVER R. YALU.

Japanese Railway

- TOKYO
- Yokohama
- Osaka
- Shimonoseki
- (ferry)
- FUSAN

Chosen Railway

- Keijyo (SEOUL)
- Shingishu
- Antung

Manchurian Railway

- To Dairen
- To Peking
- MUKDEN
- Changchun
- To Vladivo-stock
- HARBIN

TO & FROM
EUROPE
by Trans-Siberian Route

THE RAILWAY BUREAU OF THE GOVERNMENT GENERAL OF CHOSEN, Ryuzan, Chosen (Korea).
Cable Address: "SENTETS."   Code used: A.B.C., 5th Edition.

went to Mukden to travel on the Trans-Siberian to Moscow. But a more popular route, as one could then board the Trans-Siberian immediately, was via Vladivostok. That was the route taken by the Rev. Francis E. Clark, one of the first Americans to go overland round the world. He dedicated his account to the 'Never Again Society':

'No sooner had we stepped on shore than we were treated to our first disillusionment concerning Russian and the Russians. We had heard much about the terrors of the Russian customs-house. We had expected to have our baggage overhauled from turret to foundation-stone, and the feminine member of our party had pictured to herself a swarthy Cossack with sword and cutlass making hay of her belongings. . . . But our Chinese sampan-man landed us at the pier, and no customs officer appeared at the scene. We waited, but he did not come. We inquired in two or three different languages for the customs-house, but no-one knew. . . . At length, we boldly loaded our impedimenta on board a drosky, and told the driver to take it to the *Hôtel du Pacifique*. . . .

'The hotels of Vladivostok are not to be indiscriminately recommended. When Baedeker writes his inevitable guide-book about Siberia, he will not mark them with his familiar ★ unless they greatly improve upon their present condition. . . . The chief fault was that the rooms and halls were dark and dirty, and clean linen was a scarce and precious article. One sheet for each bed seemed to be the full allowance, and one small towel for three people was thought to be ample supply. When one of our party righteously complained that her towel had evidently done duty before, the Japanese chambermaid who did

Vladivostok terminus. It was here that Americans bound for Europe overland began their rail journey towards the Urals.

the English for the hotel replied that it was impossible to get another. . . .

'But the time has come for the start [of the journey across Russia]. Five minutes before the train starts a large station bell is rung. Four minutes more the passengers stroll up and down the platform and visit the buffet. Then the bell is rung once more, the conductor blows his whistle, the engine shrieks a warning blast, and at last we are off with St Petersburg 9877 versts (more than 6250 miles) away.'

And so across Siberia Clark and his party went, in the train and across the countryside described in the last chapter. Round-the-world rail travel, in which the sea voyages were mere gap-fillers, had at last become a reality with the opening of the twentieth century, and was to remain so for but little over a decade more.

Two of the Centuries
passing on their way
between New York and
Chicago.

AS THE "CENTURIES
The Twentieth C
of the NEW YORK C

11. The Twentieth Century Limited

THE NIGHT
Limited
AL LINES

Although you could travel Pullman from US cities to Canada and Mexico, there was no truly great international train in North America. Instead, by a familiar combination of publicity and genuine service, the Twentieth Century Limited of the New York Central Railroad grasped the status of America's greatest train. Not all travellers agreed, but in those days it was not the travellers, but the vast newspaper-reading public, which decided which trains were great and which were not. Which really meant that a newsworthy train became a great train as often as a great train became a newsworthy train.

The New York Central 'System' was largely the work of Commodore Vanderbilt, who quite early in his career as financier, speculator, and robber-baron made an enemy of George Pullman. One of the lines he acquired to build his system was the Michigan Central, and he raised long-living hackles among the Pullmans by replacing Pullman cars on that line with Wagner's cars; this was a blow not only to the Pullmans' business but also to their sentimentality, because the Michigan Central had been one of their earliest and most vital customers. But for many subsequent decades the Twentieth Century Limited, that joint enterprise of the New York Central and Pullman, was the showpiece of American sleeping car travel.

The railways were America's first big business, and it has often been said that they set the pattern for financing, manning, and organizing the USA's big growth industries. Never before had such large and complex undertakings been attempted, demanding new methods and new forms, and attracting a new breed of men. Of such men Cornelius Vanderbilt (1794–1877) was one of the most outstanding, and the New York Central Railroad was his best-known creation. 'Creation' is perhaps a euphemism, because over the decades it has been slowly realized

ABOVE Commodore Cornelius Vanderbilt, the robber baron who prepared the way for the Twentieth Century Limited and made a personal fortune of over $100 million.

BELOW An early de luxe coach used by travellers between New York and Chicago.

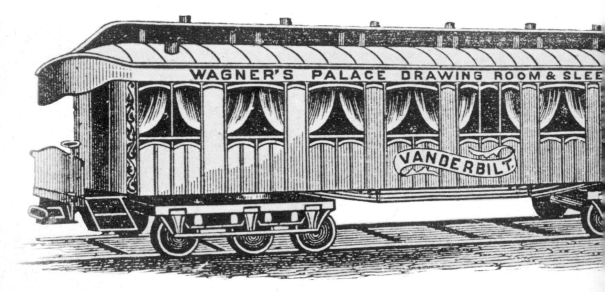

that men like Vanderbilt really created very little. Their
contemporaries may have regarded them as those ruthless and
imaginative men who were needed to build the USA into the
world's greatest economic power, but a closer look suggests
that their wealth was not created, but was simply accumulated
at the expense of others. Accumulated wealth equalled concen-
trated power, and this power enabled men of the Vanderbilt
stamp to do things which others could not do. But what they did
was not always desirable.

Like so many of the rich, shady entrepreneurs of America's
railway age, Vanderbilt was a product of the eighteenth century.
He was of humble birth and gained his commercial experience
as a ferry-boat operator between Staten Island and New York
City. Steamboats were a growing industry at this time, and he
prospered, eventually granting himself the rank of commodore
in his own Hudson river fleet. Always more far-seeing than his
rivals, he decided to invest his wealth in the railroads, which he
realized had a more dazzling future than steamboat navigation.

His first big moves in the railroad business came after the
Civil War. By this time the eastern states had all the railroads
they needed, but sharp characters like Vanderbilt could still
make fortunes by manipulating railroad shares. Vanderbilt
stands out not so much for his imagination or for the scale of his
dealings, but because he was the first large-scale practitioner of
the policy of buying-up competitors. Instead of trying to force
rival railroads into some kind of agreement, or to ruin them by
undercutting, or to block them with the help of bribable
legislators or judges, Vanderbilt had the will and the wealth to
make attractive offers for their property.

Vanderbilt started his railroad career by quietly acquiring
control of the short New York and Harlem Railroad. After he
and his friends had gained a majority of the shares they enriched
themselves by successive 'cornering' deals. At the time of
acquisition, the shares stood at 30, but Vanderbilt soon lifted
them to 285. The mechanism of cornering was simple; it
required cunning, discretion, and unscrupulousness – qualities
possessed by most denizens of Wall Street – plus nerve and
powerful financial backing. Vanderbilt merely contracted with
speculators, who anticipated a fall in the stock, to buy in the
future so many shares at current market prices. If the shares did
fall, the speculators could be sure of a killing, because Vanderbilt would have to buy at the previous higher price. What the
speculators did not know was that Vanderbilt already controlled
the shares. When the time came for them to acquire these shares
on the market, in order to re-sell them to Vanderbilt in accord-
ance with the contract, they discovered there were no shares to
be bought. Their desperate demand for shares forced up the
price, and when the shares had appreciated to what Vanderbilt
considered a good figure he sold enough shares on the market to

enable his victims to fulfill their contract. In due course they presented him with the same shares, for which he paid the low, previously agreed, price. He managed to pull off this manoeuvre several times. Daniel Drew, his future rival, was one of his victims; he was scorched to the tune of half a million dollars and never forgot it.

The wealth amassed by these cornering operations helped Vanderbilt to buy his next acquisition, the Hudson River Railroad. This picturesque line along the Hudson ran from New York to Albany and would later develop into the four-track 'water level' line of the New York Central.

At that time the New York Central was a line across the state of New York to Buffalo, and it was not long before Vanderbilt got hold of this too. Then, by adding to his 'system' the Lake Shore and Michigan Southern, which ran from Buffalo westwards, Vanderbilt achieved his ambition of being in a position to run trains on his own tracks all the way from New York to Chicago. In economic and social terms this was Vanderbilt's only achievement: the welding of a collection of small lines into a trunk route connecting America's two biggest cities. There is no reason to believe that if Vanderbilt had not achieved this, somebody else would not have done so. And this somebody else would probably not have extracted so high a price from society for doing it; Vanderbilt is believed to be the first American to chalk up a hundred-million dollar personal fortune.

In his quest for personal wealth Vanderbilt was not content to control merely his trunk line. He soon set his sights on the Erie Railroad, which also provided a service westwards from New York. Once he had the Erie he would have a monopoly of New York railroads, and could raise his fares and tariffs to a fortune-making level. But the treasurer and virtual controller of the Erie was Daniel Drew, his arch-enemy.

A one-time cattle boy, later a tavern keeper, Drew was a much cruder type of operator. His interest in the railroad business had brought him in due course the post of treasurer of the Erie Railroad. He hatched most of his spectacular and much-admired coups in his Wall Street office; by this time New York's Wall Street was establishing itself as America's financial centre, to the detriment of its rivals in Boston and Philadelphia. In general, Drew made his fortune by enriching himself at the expense of the Erie shareholders, while from time to time exerting noble and inspired efforts to save the Erie from ruin; after all, geese which lay golden eggs should be preserved.

While Vanderbilt was building up his New York Central System, Drew's Erie Railroad was facing a crippling cash shortage. Drew devised a classic rescue operation. From his own pocket (whose contents had been amassed earlier at the expense of the Railroad) he made a loan to the Company, taking several

An early advertisement for Vanderbilt's passenger services.

million dollars' worth of Erie shares as security. This deal was kept quiet, and Drew then made contracts with speculators, who agreed to buy Erie stock from Drew in the future, at current prices. At the time, Erie stock was rising, partly thanks to the cash loan which Drew had inconspicuously made to the Railroad. Thus the speculators had every reason to believe that they were on to a good thing. But when the time approached for Drew to deliver the stock which he had promised, he sold his recently and secretly acquired shares on the market. This sudden flood virtually halved the price, thereby enabling Drew to achieve the most complete triumph of his financial life. He could buy back the shares cheaply, and then sell them to the speculators, who were obliged to pay the previous, higher, price. After this, Drew temporarily withdrew from the limelight, but his coup was long remembered. It was about this time that the Erie began to be known as 'the scarlet woman of Wall Street'.

Determined to acquire the Erie, but knowing that Drew would oppose him, Vanderbilt first had recourse to the courts. He realized that if he or his nominees tried to buy a controlling block of Erie shares Drew would merely issue new shares so that a majority holding would never be acquired. Vanderbilt succeeded in persuading a New York Supreme Court judge to grant a temporary injunction preventing the Erie issuing new shares. Having, as he thought, thereby secured his flank, he began to make generous offers for Erie shares on the Wall Street market. Erie shares rose, even though an unexpected block of shares was placed on the market. Vanderbilt gobbled up these, only to discover that they were fresh from the printers; defying the courts, the Erie had issued new shares, and several millions of Vanderbilt's dollars had disappeared into the coffers of the Erie.

What followed was described by Charles F. Adams in his *A Chapter of Erie* (1871):

'The morning of the 11th found the Erie leaders still transacting business at the office of the corporation in Wall Street. It would seem that these gentlemen, in spite of the glaring contempt for the process of the courts of which they had been guilty, had made no arrangements for an orderly retreat beyond the jurisdiction of the tribunals they had set at defiance. They were speedily roused from their real or affected tranquillity by trustworthy intelligence that processes for contempt were already issued against them, and that their only chance of escape from incarceration lay in precipitate flight. At ten o'clock the astonished police saw a throng of panic-stricken railway directors – looking more like a gang of thieves, disturbed in the division of their plunder, than like the wealthy representatives of a great corporation – rush headlong from the doors of the Erie office, and dash off in the direction of the Jersey ferry. In their hands were packages and files of papers, and their pockets

ROUTE 1843.

Buffalo.

MMENCE JULY 10 1843.

uffalo, - $10. in the best cars,
  8. in accomodation cars,
ushioned and lighted.
hester, $8. in the best cars.
  6.50 in accomodation cars.

Y LINES.

25 hours.

GOING EAST.

	1st Train	2d Train	3d Train
e Buffalo,	4 A.M.	9 A.M.	4 P.M.
Rochester,	9 A.M.	3 P.M.	10 P.M.
Auburn,	3 P.M.	9 P.M.	4 A.M.
Syracuse,	5 P.M.	11 P.M.	6 A.M.
Utica,	9 P.M.	4 A.M.	10 A.M.
Schenectady,	3 A.M.	10 A.M.	3 P.M.
e at Albany,	5 A.M.	11 A.M.	4 P.M.

BY SPECIAL CONTRACT.

at Albany, Buffalo or Rochester
the reduced rates.
ve places to any other places
te.

were crammed with assets and securities. One individual bore away with him in a hackney-coach bales containing six millions of dollars in greenbacks. Other members of the board followed under cover of the night; some of them, not daring to expose themselves to the publicity of a ferry, attempted to cross in open boats concealed by the darkness and a March fog. Two directors, who lingered, were arrested; but a majority of the Executive Committee collected at the Erie Station in Jersey City, and there, free from any apprehension of Judge Barnard's pursuing wrath, proceeded to the transaction of business.

'Meanwhile, on the other side of the river, Vanderbilt was struggling in the toils. As usual in these Wall Street operations, there was a grim humour in the situation. Had Vanderbilt failed to sustain the market, a financial collapse and panic must have ensued which would have sent him to the wall.'

Vanderbilt's empire, his New York Central System, was laden with millions of dollars-worth of falling Erie shares and was in danger of collapse. If Vanderbilt collapsed, so would Wall Street, and it was perhaps this which enabled the Commodore to get the financial resources he needed to weather this storm. He was not beaten, and still intended to get hold of the Erie.

Resort to the courts had proved a failure, but he had intimate ties with the legislature. So the scene was shifted to Albany, the state capital. Here a highly profitable senate committee began to enquire into the affairs of the Erie Railroad. Largely because Vanderbilt's men were more skilled and generous in bribing the senators, the final report of the committee condemned the Drew party. This was a great success for Vanderbilt; although his aim was to establish a monopoly detrimental to the state of New York, he had persuaded that state's legislature, and its newspapers, to support him.

But the Drew party did not give in. Accusing Vanderbilt of monopoly, the Erie men cut their freight rates by a third in order to undercut the New York Central, a move which won them much public acclaim. So far did public opinion move in their favour that they persuaded the legislators to pass a bill confirming the Erie's right to issue new stock.

This put an end to Vanderbilt's ambition. As he said, he could always find money to buy the Erie Railroad, but he could never find enough to buy its printing press. A New York judge commented that the state legislature had presented the Erie with a licence to print counterfeit money, but this comment did not help Vanderbilt. Thus the New York Central system never got a monopoly of the New York to Chicago service, and in due course had to enter into genuine competition with rival lines. It was out of this competition that fine trains like the Twentieth Century Limited would emerge.

Commodore Vanderbilt died soon afterwards, and was succeeded by his son William. William was less firm than his father, had a fat body and fat side-whiskers, and was more interested in horses than in railways. Afraid of political attacks on him, he decided to relinquish his control of the New York Central by reducing his shareholding. To do this he turned to the most celebrated of the new class of railroad organizer, the investment banker J. Pierpont Morgan. Morgan duly sold the shares on the London market, and then returned to his other endeavours. Having channelled so much of his clients' money into railroads, he wanted them to succeed, and tried to help when they seemed in danger. One of his first successful rescue operations concerned the New York Central. Commodore Vanderbilt's practice of buying out competitors had already had its natural outcome: new railroads built simply for sale to the existing lines whose profits they threatened. The New York Central had already been obliged to spend millions on buying out the Nickel Plate Railroad, which had been built parallel to it from Buffalo to Chicago.

Now another line was being built to threaten the New York Central. This was the West Shore line from New York to Buffalo, one of whose backers was George Pullman, still bearing a grudge against the Vanderbilts. Meanwhile, William Vanderbilt, abetted by Andrew Carnegie, was building a line from Pittsburgh to embarrass another competitor in the New York to Chicago service, the Pennsylvania Railroad.

J. Pierpont Morgan was well aware how costly these manoeuvres were to railroad shareholders. Indeed, it was at this period that the eastern states were being saddled with that multiplicity of unnecessary railroads which absorbed money which would have been better spent in other undertakings and which today still exists as a millstone around the neck of the ailing railroad companies. But in this particular case, by inviting the contestants on board his yacht and plying them with endless alcohol and argument, he arranged for Vanderbilt to buy up the West Shore on favourable terms while giving up his Pittsburgh line to the Pennsylvania Railroad.

After this, the New York Central and its rivals evidently decided that their energies would henceforth be devoted less to backroom financial manoeuvring and beggar-my-neighbour coups, and more to an improvement of their services. At long last the benefits of the competitive system were to be presented to a long-suffering public. It was no accident therefore that the turn of the century witnessed a new era in passenger train service. Of the new services the Twentieth Century Limited was destined to become the most celebrated. Not perhaps the most typical, but the most-quoted example of American trains at their best.

Between New York and Chicago at one time there were eleven different railway routes offered to the passenger, one of them via Canada. But as the decades passed it was the Pennsylvania and New York Central which were the major contenders for this traffic, with their crack Broadway Limited and Twentieth Century Limited. Even in its year of inauguration, thanks to masterly publicity, the Twentieth Century Limited gained a world-wide reputation as America's greatest train. One New York paper once demanded that since the Twentieth Century Limited had become such a magnificent name it should always be printed in capital letters.

Although the Twentieth Century Limited only began running in 1902, it was in the nineties that the New York Central first began to operate its family of crack trains. The stimulus was the Chicago Columbian Exposition of 1893, during which the Railroad ran its Exposition Flyer from New York on an unprecedented schedule of twenty hours for the 960 miles. At the Exposition itself, the alliance of the New York Central with Wagner's sleeping car company was further cemented by the exhibition train shown jointly by these two companies. A few years later a fast train very similar to the exhibition train was put into service between New York and Chicago. In this the combination of railway and Wagner reached its climax. The train consisted of seven long (eighty-foot) cars, of which three cars provided berths (and revenue) while the other four were designed to lure customers. There was a library/smoker, a luxurious diner, all tassel and plush, a parlor car and, at the rear, an observation car with the traditional open platform. The whole train had two sets of lighting, conventional gas lamps and much more novel electric lights.

Only the best of Wagner's porters and maids were employed in this service, and they all carried a copy of Wagner's *Rules for Uniformed Employees*, one of whose rules was that each employee should carry a copy of Wagner's *Rules for Uniformed Employees*. The male attendants, while relieved of the maids' obligation to carry on their person smelling salts, needles, and pins, were strictly enjoined not to present that 'decidedly loafering appearance' which came from putting their hands in their overcoat tails during cold weather.

The New York Central by this time was run by businessmen rather than by get-rich-quick manipulators. Its passenger agent, George Daniels, was the architect of the Railroad's sudden status as a standard-setter for passenger services. Daniels was a one-time patent medicine saleman, who only came into his own after joining the railway. It was he who introduced the red-cap station porters, who soon became the hallmark of US railroads. A born showman, he pulled off an unusual publicity coup at this time.

The American public was still in a state of rapturous intoxication following the Spanish-American War, and a modest magazine had published an equally modest piece called *A Message to Garcia*, which unexpectedly became a sellout. *A Message to*

Garcia was about a man who, given a seemingly impossible task (carrying a message from Theodore Roosevelt to a holed-up-in-the-jungle Cuban general), simply said he would do it, and did. This uplifting piece delighted all those who felt that every American worker needed to be shown what it meant to be a good worker. Everybody, even including some workers, wanted to read it. Daniels had the piece reprinted as a pamphlet, with an advertisement of his passenger train service on the back, and distributed over a million copies to his passengers and fellow-citizens.

The Russian Prince Khilkov was inspecting the New York Central at this time, and ordered a translation for the benefit of Russian railway workers. Khilkov was also interested in Daniels's crack trains, but when he got back to Russia his task as Minister of Transport would be, not the running of crack trains, but the reorganization of the Trans-Siberian Railway to enable it to carry the reinforcements needed by the army in its war against Japan in 1904.

Daniels's biggest success was his Twentieth Century Limited. The name itself almost guaranteed success, for the American public still remembered the joys and celebrations of 1 January 1900, when one century was cast off for another, a new century which would surely be America's century.

The first run was on 15 June 1902. The twenty-hour schedule was perhaps unexciting by 1902, but the luxury of the train set (or was said to set) new standards. With five cars, there was accommodation for forty-two passengers; obviously with a ratio of eight passengers per car there was plenty of scope for extravagant spaciousness. On this first trip there were in fact only twenty-seven passengers, of whom the most notable was a wealthy character known as John 'Bet-a-Million' Gates. Gates commented that the new train had turned Chicago into a suburb of New York, a compliment which did not go down too well with Chicagoans.

Despite the supplementary fare which was charged, the Twentieth Century Limited with its forty-two berths could hardly be a money-making train. It is doubtful whether it ever became a profit-maker; in the twenties, when it was a much longer train, it was said to be highly profitable. But railway cost accounting is notoriously flexible; depending on what assumptions are made, a given train can be shown to be highly profitable or highly unprofitable. How the cost of track and signalling and buildings is split between freight and passenger services makes a crucial difference to the appearance of passenger service accounts, a fact which was duly exploited by the passenger train enthusiasts in the thirties, and by the passenger trains' enemies in the sixties. Certainly the ratio of passengers per car of trains like the Twentieth Century Limited was far below what nowadays would be considered a viable figure.

Still, whether or not it made an operating profit, the Twentieth Century Limited worked wonders for the image both of the New York Central and of American passenger trains in general. By making long distance train travel an apparently pleasurable and fashionable activity, rather than a necessity, this new image must have boosted the passenger traffic of all railways offering sleeper services.

By this time the Wagner Company had been taken over by the Pullman Company and the Wagner cars used on the Century had been refurbished by the latter. But although the so-called Gothic lights, and a scattering of oval stained-glass windows, may have impressed contemporaries, the exterior paintwork in what was euphemistically described as Pullman Green was certainly not an aesthetic success. This drab paint, a kind of olive which gradually turned black, disfigured most US sleeping car trains up to the diesel era. Only a few lines insisted on their own colours, as the Pennsylvania did with its maroon and gold. However, the interior appointments of the Century's cars were more important than the dull exterior and when, in 1904, the

train was re-equipped with specially built Pullmans it was well on the road to a fond place in American hearts.

This was a time when the steam railway was approaching the peak of its grip on popular imagination. The Editor of the *Scientific American* was on to a good thing when he wrote for his 1902 *Transportation Supplement* a description of a footplate trip on the Century:

'. . . We have stood at night on the bridge of the *Deutschland* when, with the *Kaiser Wilhelm* at her heels she was rushing at twenty-seven miles an hour through a fog that shut the forecastle deck from view; and again when, to test her rough-weather ability, she was making twenty-four miles an hour against a full southwesterly gale; but from the standpoint of pure sensationalism those experiences were tame compared to this wild ride by night through the Mohawk Valley. To the writer, who was not by any means a stranger to locomotive riding, the experience was simply terrific – impossible of adequate description to the traveller whose gauge of greater speed is the slightly increased swaying of a Pullman car. The sensations of such a ride

Grand Central Station on 46th Street, New York, 1907: the starting point of the Twentieth Century Limited.

strike at every avenue to the emotions; ear, eye, and touch are violently assailed. For the ear there is a "clang and clash and roar", so loud that one has to shout into the ear to be heard – there is the concussion of the moving parts of the engine – the jangling of metal against metal – the crashing impact of the driving wheels and trailers upon the track – while above all this strident orchestra, like some great organ note, is heard the deep, sustained roar of the exhaust from the smokestack. For the sense of touch there is the amazingly rough riding of the engine which, compared with a nicely-poised Pullman car, is as the movement of a springless farm wagon to a rubber-tired carriage. The unevenness of the track, slight as it is, is but little absorbed by the stiff locomotive springs, and when the driving wheels and the massive reciprocating parts – side rods, connecting rods, crossheads, pistons, weighing tons in the aggregate – are threshing round and darting to and fro to the tune of three hundred revolutions a minute, the great mass of the engine vibrates and lurches and rolls, until one feels that the only logical outcome would be for the structure to rend itself into a thousand fragments! . . .'

Still intent on emphasizing the contrast between the pampered existence inside a Pullman car and the rough, exposed, and heroic life on the locomotive, the writer continued: 'To the novice, the most thrilling moments come with the headlong dash through a station yard, where the tail-lights of a side-tracked freight train glare with their evil red eyes at you from the distance – surely they are on your own track – and you sweep down upon a mass of white lights, red lights, headlights, whirling above, with two or three switching locomotives to heighten the crowded effect! Clear track? Absurdly impossible! I tell you, gentle passenger, lounging back there in the cushioned security and comfort of a Pullman, that should you sit here just now with me at the very front end of this roaring cataract of steel and fire, and realize that it is hurling you into that bewildering yard at over one hundred feet a second, with a stored-up energy back of you equal to that of a shell from a thirteen-inch gun – if you realized, as I did, that to develop that energy requires only a misplaced switch, a careless signalman, a broken rail or axle, you would understand how sublime must be the faith of that quiet man at the throttle (whose clean-cut profile you can just see silhouetted against the window of his cab) in the material, the men, and the management of that most wonderful of modern creations, a first-class trunk railroad . . .

'It is a popular delusion that the engineers who run such trains soon break down under the strain; yet the two partners on the New York–Albany run of this train are to-day fine-looking men in the best of health. The work calls for nerve, of course, but as more than one of them told us, they kept their nerves right by right living. A more temperate, intelligent, and courteous body of men than these one must travel far to find . . .'

On the trip just described, the load was three hundred tons, not a heavy train by US standards. Some time was lost at Syracuse; the New York Central's line passed along the main street, and as it was election night there were enough revellers thronging the tracks to force the pride and glory of American passenger trains down to a crawl, instead of the usual cautious stroll through the city. In regaining the lost time, a maximum of eighty-three mph was timed by the editor-reporter against the mileposts; as elsewhere in the world, American locomotives had no speedometers. Probably that eighty-three mph was not a record for the train. A few days after its inauguration it had been delayed en route for two and a half hours and the management, very sensitive about adverse publicity, ordered nearly five hundred miles of track to be cleared to give the train a chance to recover the loss. What speed was reached is unknown, but it is known that 481 miles were covered in 460 minutes, and arrival in Chicago was only half an hour late. A few years earlier a New Central train had reached 112 mph and its engine, no. 999, was rewarded with a permanent resting place inside a museum.

On the eve of the First World War the Century's schedule was down to eighteen hours, like that of its rival, the Broadway Limited. Its old wooden cars had been replaced by all-steel vehicles; when the other crack trains had been similarly re-equipped, yet another advertising slogan was born, 'The All-Steel Fleet'. But at first the all-steel cars did not meet with universal approval. In fact, some of the Century's steel cars had their side panels grained to resemble wood, apparently to re-assure those passengers who believed that steel cars attracted lightning. Among the on-train services provided by the Pullman Company and its attendants were a barber shop, manicurist, stenographer, stock market reports, valets, ladies' maids, and bathrooms supplied both with fresh water and salt water.

But probably the Twentieth Century Limited's finest period was the twenties and thirties. In the late twenties neither the automobile nor the aeroplane had made much inroad into the long-distance passenger market. The slight annual fall in rail passengers was ascribed to the increasing use of the long-distance telephone, and this fall was not reflected in the demand for luxury train services. In those days the Century was almost always operated in several sections, and in 1928 a record 225,000 tickets were sold.

In the Christmas period, five separate Centurys were often run in each direction. At such times New York Central photographers would descend on the terminus at Chicago to photograph the several sections lined up ready to leave. Grand Central Terminus at the New York end, grandiose though it might be in its concourse, did not lend itself to this photographic exercise, for its platforms were subterranean and devoid of photogenic snow and steam.

The record came in January 1929, when on one day no fewer than seven sections followed each other out of Chicago. But these seven trains only carried a total of 822 passengers, a number which despite the ten-dollar surcharge would not be regarded as especially profitable nowadays. In 1926 the Century brought in ten million dollars, but this was its gross income, and at that time two dozen locomotives and about 120 cars were used for this service, together with their crews. Still, profit or no profit, few Americans now doubted that it was 'The Greatest Train in the World' (another advertising slogan). However, by mutual agreement the eighteen-hour schedules of the Broadway and the Century had been slowed down to the former 20 hours.

By the early thirties the train usually consisted of twelve or thirteen Pullman cars, and left New York in mid-afternoon in order to arrive in Chicago the next morning. That special mark of the Century, a train-long red carpet rolled out on to the platform each day, was designed to give the passengers a foretaste of luxury as they made their way to their reserved accommodation. The first six minutes of the journey were spent in tunnels beneath New York City, and then the train emerged into the open at Harlem. For the first three-quarters of an hour, to Harmon, the traction was electric, but for the remainder of the picturesque ride northwards beside the broad Hudson river a powerful steam locomotive, of a wheel arrangement christened by the New York Central as the Hudson Type, was in charge of the train.

Because the route lay mainly in the valleys of the Hudson and Mohawk, and along the shore of the Great Lakes, the New York Central had full justification for its best-known slogan, proudly calling itself 'The Water Level Route'. Usually it went a little further than this in its passenger train advertisements. 'The Water Level Route – You Can Sleep' was an obvious dig at the

rival Pennsylvania Railroad, whose Chicago trains crossed the Alleghenies at quite a high altitude and therefore, in the minds of advertising copywriters, could not possibly provide so smooth a ride.

Maximum permitted speed up to Albany was sixty-five mph, and this had to be reduced to forty-five mph when water was scooped up from the track troughs. At Albany the engine crew was changed, and two Pullman cars from the Boston line were added. At Syracuse the dining car was dropped, and a little further on the train stopped with the locomotive beneath a coal gantry astride the tracks. Taking on thirty tons of coal took only a minute or two, and the same engine was enabled to continue to the outskirts of Cleveland, with another change of crew at Buffalo. Thus the first of the westbound Century's two steam locomotives covered 581 miles, averaging about 55 mph. Cleveland, like New York, did not tolerate locomotive smoke, so the train was hauled by an electric locomotive through that city, with a fresh Hudson steam engine waiting to be attached on the western outskirts. In the morning, at Toledo, two dining cars were picked up to provide the passengers' breakfast, and arrival at Chicago was scheduled for 9.19 Central Time. The return trip was similar, but was sometimes enlivened by the circumstance that for several miles out of Chicago the eastbound Century and Broadway were scheduled to run neck-and-neck over parallel tracks.

This was the period when streamlining hit the railroads. To justify what was really only a publicity gimmick, the New York Central stressed that there was a prevailing westerly wind over its main line. It then shrouded one of its Hudson locomotives, the 'Commodore Vanderbilt', in a smooth cover, rather resembling an upturned bathtub, and repeated the process with a handful of other locomotives. However, in 1938 this unprepossessing experiment was overtaken by four completely new trains designed for the Twentieth Century Limited service.

Streamlined locomotives which hauled passenger trains across the USA.

These had been expensively styled by a well-known industrial designer, Dreyfuss, and the locomotives were given bullet noses and smooth side panels.

For these four trains, sixty-two new cars and ten new engines were built. 'Pullman Green' had been abandoned, and the new trains were enhanced by a livery of grey, blue and silver. But from the passengers' point of view the main change was that this was the 'First All-Room Train in America', meaning that Pullman's traditional open sleeping car design had been abandoned in favour of a train in which every berth was in a compartment. Thus from an 'All-Sleeper' train the Century had risen to the new status of 'No Open-Berth' train. Moreover, its schedule was now only of sixteen hours.

This 1938 edition of the Century probably represents the peak of its career from the equipment point of view. In 1948, now described by the New York Central publicists as 'The Favorite

ABOVE RIGHT A modern view of the interior of the Twentieth Century Limited. The train was taken out of the timetable in 1967.

RIGHT One of the locomotives which hauled the Twentieth Century Limited, 1941.

Train of Famous People', the post-war Century was inaugurated at a ceremony in Grand Central Station by Dwight D. Eisenhower and Beatrice Lillie. The champagne bottle smashed on the tail of the observation car was said to be filled symbolically with water taken from the Hudson, Mohawk, and the Great Lakes. The new trains were painted in two tones of grey, with white lining. Although time-honoured features like open-ended observation cars had long disappeared, these had been more than replaced, at least in the opinion of the copywriters, by such modern marvels as fluorescent lighting and foam rubber mattresses.

A postwar innovation was the attachment of through cars to Los Angeles and San Francisco. Many years previously, a critic of the fact that there were no through passenger trains between the eastern and western states, but plenty of through freight services, declared that US railroads made travel easier for pigs than for people. Evidently this would no longer be true: passengers who could afford private rooms in the trains would now receive equal treatment with pigs, at least as far as changing trains at Chicago was concerned.

But in general the post-war years were not good years either for railway passenger services or for Pullman. The aeroplane and the automobile had well and truly arrived. In 1958 the unheard-of was heard: the New York Central announced that the Twentieth Century Limited would henceforth also carry sitting passengers. Although the publicists made great play with clever phrases about the luxuries of great trains being brought within the reach of the less well-off, a nation which was already satiated with the language of advertising never really believed this yarn; a train available to all was obviously no longer entitled to be regarded as an exclusive train. In the following decade those two competitors, the New York Central and the Pennsylvania railroads, joined forces in the hope that two deficits might equal one profit. This was a vain hope, and in 1967 the Twentieth Century Limited, said to be making heavy losses, was taken out of the timetable. Not many Americans missed it, but those who did shook their heads and spoke of the end of an era.

12. Where are the Trains of Yesteryear?

The Indian-Pacific, perhaps destined to be the last great train to be brought into service. Linking Perth with Sydney, its comforts and accommodation are comparable with those of nineteenth-century trains.

Georges Nagelmackers died in his chateau at Villepreux, near Paris, in 1905; and the era of great international *trains de luxe* did not long survive him. It is the purpose of this final chapter to suggest that it may even now be returning.

The First World War broke out less than a decade after Nagelmackers's death, and brought La Compagnie Internationale's operations to a virtual standstill. The Bolshevik revolution and other political traumas which followed meant that the overland route to the Far East and around the world was cut off, as it effectively has been ever since.

Even those expresses of Nagelmackers's creation that were brought back into service were not the same again. Quite simply, the class for whom they had been created had fallen from grace during the war and its aftermath.

La Compagnie Internationale's new Director-General was an Englishman, Lord Dalziel. He had made his first fortune by introducing motor taxi-cabs into service in London, and had then become agent in Britain for La Compagnie Internationale. The Dalziels' ties with the Nagelmackers were close – his daughter had married Georges's son, although she had died soon after. Dalziel was an outstanding businessman, but even had he possessed Nagelmackers's sense of style and spirit of adventure, these might only have served to put him out of step with his time.

No longer, under his command, was it the business of La Compagnie Internationale to carry a select few in conditions of luxury and elegance across continents to remote and exotic destinations. It was now to carry larger numbers in less comfort and for less money to holiday resorts nearer home. To pursue his profitable, but scarcely romantic, objective Dalziel acquired control of Thomas Cook and Sons Ltd and of the English Pullman Company, and merged them into La Compagnie Internationale, thus forming a near-monopoly of foreign travel within Europe.

Having consolidated his position, standards were allowed to decline. The opulent coaches of Nagelmackers's time, carrying as few as twelve people in private coupés were withdrawn from service, and replaced by the open Pullman cars pre-war Europe had so scornfully spurned. The new passengers no longer dressed for dinner, which had in any case been reduced to a mere soup, meat and dessert affair. Such luxuries as smoking rooms, ladies' salons, libraries and bathrooms were dispensed with, for they took up space on trains that could be occupied by fare-paying passengers. As for the Palace hotels so lovingly and lavishly founded by Nagelmackers, Dalziel simply failed to reopen them. It was some compensation, however, that the Athénée Palace in Paris, the Avenida Palace in Lisbon and the Palace in Madrid were all sold to new proprietors who did respect and maintain their traditions for the depleted ranks of travellers who could still afford to stay in them.

Lord Dalziel, who became Director-General of La Compagnie Internationale in 1926.

The Second World War brought La Compagnie Internationale's operations to a standstill again, and afterwards its career was still more troubled than in the years that had followed the First World War. American holidaymakers by and large stayed away from Europe for several years. The British, who had been the company's greatest source of custom throughout its history, were restricted by the government in the amount of foreign currency they might spend on travel abroad, initially to twenty-five pounds per person per year.

This necessary austerity measure had two consequences. First, and most obviously, it ruled out any possibility of indulgence in first-class rail travel, even of the reduced standards of comfort Dalziel had provided. Second and less obviously, it alerted large numbers of people who had previously ignored the possibility of foreign travel as being too expensive an undertaking, to the fact that it could be indulged in at very little cost. So many of them began to go abroad for the first time that the whole character of Europe for visitors was changed – those who remembered it before agreed for the worse.

As private coupés had given way to four-berth sleeping compartments thirty-five years before, so now the latter were replaced in many cases by banks of couchettes, eight to each section. The hard, narrow bunks affording very little privacy or headroom, where passengers bedded down in their day clothes without regard to sex, were indeed reminiscent of the conditions that had so shocked and depressed Nagelmackers during his visit to the United States in the 1840s. The wheel had turned full circle: and as for meals, these were now in many cases dispensed from mobile snack trolleys moving along the corridors laden with beer, coffee, soft drinks and large, unbuttered and sparsely-filled sandwiches.

Even when the restrictions on foreign currency for travel abroad were relaxed, things did not much improve. The pattern was set. Chartered trains of wagons-couchettes lined up at Calais Maritime station to take on board the tourist hordes disgorged from the overcrowded channel ferries. Then they trundled their way down Europe to a Mediterranean coast now lined with holiday encampments. The seeds for the destruction of international travel had been sown.

In the 1950s the economics of travel suddenly changed in favour of the aeroplane. What had happened was that the introduction of passenger jets into scheduled service dramatically reduced the value of propeller-driven aircraft almost overnight, making them available for special flights for holidaymakers. Faced with a choice of three or four hours' discomfort in the air or perhaps thirty-six hours of discomfort on a train, few opted for the latter.

The change that had taken place was more remarkable and sadder than the bare facts convey. An exciting reality of foreign travel that Nagelmackers had offered had been substituted by what amounted to little more than a drab illusion. It was a process fostered by a change in the nature of the men who ran the travel business, from travellers to marketing experts. These latter might as well have been selling lipsticks or household cleansers as holidays, and in some cases had been doing so previously.

The theory on which they based their approach was a little-publicized and thoroughly uncongenial one that deserved to fail, as it seemed it had done by the winter of 1974 and 1975. It was the theory that modern-day travellers did not much enjoy the experience of being abroad. They went in order to fantasize and boast about it before and afterwards, the argument ran. Therefore, what one was selling was not a set of physical services – transport, hotel accommodation, meals and the like – but a kind of dream to be indulged in for twenty-five weeks before the event and twenty-five afterwards, the two weeks of holiday in the middle being nearly irrelevant.

Money was lavished on fostering the dream through television commercials, brochures and other forms of publicity, arguably at the expense of the quality of the holiday itself. It seemed that the theory was wrong: after the initial excitement of the new age of travel had worn off people stayed away from it in ever larger numbers and many travel firms went bankrupt.

With hindsight, it is not hard to see where the error lay. It was not the case that people found little pleasure in going abroad because it was not potentially an enjoyable experience. It was that it had not been made to be an enjoyable experience any longer. Trains had not declined in popularity because the aircraft offered an inherently superior form of travel. Such a proposition is patently absurd. Rail travel is potentially more comfortable by far than air travel can ever be, as Nagelmackers demonstrated with such flair in the nineteenth century. On board, one can move about, eat, drink and sleep in some luxury, as well as greater safety. Furthermore, one has the agreeable sensation of travelling, a sensation of which air travel robs one – one passes through towns and villages and the countryside and observes the life by the side of the track. In the air, one does not.

Travellers were never given an opportunity of showing which form of conveyance they preferred, for the choice of a proper train, in the sense that Nagelmackers's were, was no longer available to them.

There is one instance in which it has been, and the experiment has been a triumphant success. Ironically, perhaps, it has taken place in Australia, the country where civil aviation was pioneered. In 1970, the year in which the state-owned airline, Qantas, celebrated its silver jubilee, a *train de luxe* was inaugurated to link Perth with Sydney, 2,400 miles away. Called the 'Indian-Pacific', after the two oceans between whose shores it runs, it completes the journey in sixty-five hours, or about eight times longer than it takes by air.

It is a train that would probably have impressed Nagelmackers himself. Passengers ride in private apartments, to which private showers and toilet facilities are attached. Half a mile in length, the train contains an observation lounge, a drawing room, a music room with a proper piano, a cocktail bar presided over by an alumnus of Gleneagles Hotel in Scotland and restaurant cars where five-course meals of some luxury are served.

Despite the discrepancy in speeds, the Indian-Pacific has dramatically shown its ability to compete for custom against aircraft. Before the train came into service – an event celebrated with a public holiday in Perth – sixteen thousand people had made advance bookings to board it. Since then, its popularity has not flagged. In the 1960s the numbers of people who travelled between Perth and eastern Australia by train was about a seventh of those who went by air. Since the express has come into service, the numbers have increased so that at the time of writing, they are about equal. The lesson is that there are still many people who will find the time to travel by train rather than by air, if they are given a realistic choice.

It is a lesson that cannot be ignored by European railway administrations – not least by the still-flourishing La Compagnie Internationale itself, which today devotes much of its energy to catering at airports and on motorways.

There has been a major rebellion against the squalor of modern travel, and it is clear that the means of persuading the educated and the affluent to go abroad again, in the manner that they did in Nagelmackers's day, is to restore rail services to their old grandeur. In the United States, trains are coming back into favour again. Amtrak, the Government's passenger train operation, has perhaps made too much of its alleged successes in re-introducing the expresses of the past. Complaints are many and disappointments perhaps more. That is better than the action of British and French railways, at least, in withdrawing the Golden Arrow, successor to Nagelmackers's Club Train, from service between London and Paris at the very time when the rebellion against air travel was gathering force.

What is today known as the Orient Express is an international disgrace. Without so much as a restaurant car for much of its journey, it serves largely to convey Greek, Turkish and Yugoslav *Gastarbeiter* to and from Germany, in conditions of considerable squalor and unruliness. Many have ridden the train in the unfulfillable hope of recapturing a little of its former greatness.

Yet if the Orient Express were restored to its old grandeur, as the first among *trains de luxe*, it is likely that thousands would seek to travel on it for the same reason our forefathers did – for the joy of the journey.

It may yet happen all over again, by popular demand.

Acknowledgments

Photographs and illustrations were supplied by, or are reproduced by kind permission of the following (numbers in italic indicate colour illustrations). The picture on pages 144–5 by gracious permission of H.M. the Queen.

Australian Embassy: 228–9; Bettman Archive, New York: 30–1, 33, 46–7, 47, 226–7; British Museum: 18, 104–5, *198–9*; British Museum (photography by John Freeman): 57, 110, 112, 118(*right*), 120, 121, 128(*left*), 130, 131(*left*), 142, 144, 146, 155, 166(*below*), 207; British Transport Museum: *28, 54*; Canadian Pacific: 188–9, 191, 194–5, *197*; Chicago Historical Society: *26*, 45; Compagnie Internationale des Wagon-Lits: 10–11, 12–13, 14(*above*), 16, 17, 22(*above*), 22–3, 32, 50–1, 52, *53*, 59(*above & below*), *71*, 78–9, 99, 101, 103, 124, 128(*right*), 162–3, 164–5(*below*), 166(*above left & right*), 167, 180–1(*above*), *200*, 230–1; Thomas Cook & Son: 95, 96, 97, 118(*left*); William H. Coverdale Collection: *25*; Esso: 67; Galerie Charpentier: 125; Miss C. Gray: 170, 172, 174, 176–7(*below*), 180–1(*below*), 186–7; Howard Loxton: 83, 84, 190–1; India Office Library: 153, 160–1; International Society for Educational Information Tokyo: 202–3(*below*), 204, 206; Japanese Embassy: *114–15, 116*; Lords Gallery: 131(*right*), 148–9; Mansell Collection: 88, 91, 106, 107, 108–9, 109, 132–3, 136–7, 139, 140, 150–1, 154, 176, 196, 202, 202–3(*above*); Mary Evans: 14(*below*), 38–9, 42, 55, 77, 92, 93, 208; National Army Museum: 157, 160; Kenneth M. Nauman: 48(*right*); Ed Nowak: 68, 210–11, 212, 214–15, 220–1, 224–5; Novosti Press Agency: 168–9; Paul Popper: 12–13, 122–3; Pullman: 44–5; Radio Times Hulton Picture Library: 81, 179, 212–13; Snark International: 62–3, *72*, 164–5, 170–1, 176–7; Dr Ransome Wallis: 226; Union Pacific Railroad Museum Collection: 48(*left*); Victoria and Albert Museum: 126; Weidenfeld and Nicolson archive: *113*.

Picture research by Philippa Lewis and Juliet Scott.

Index

Index

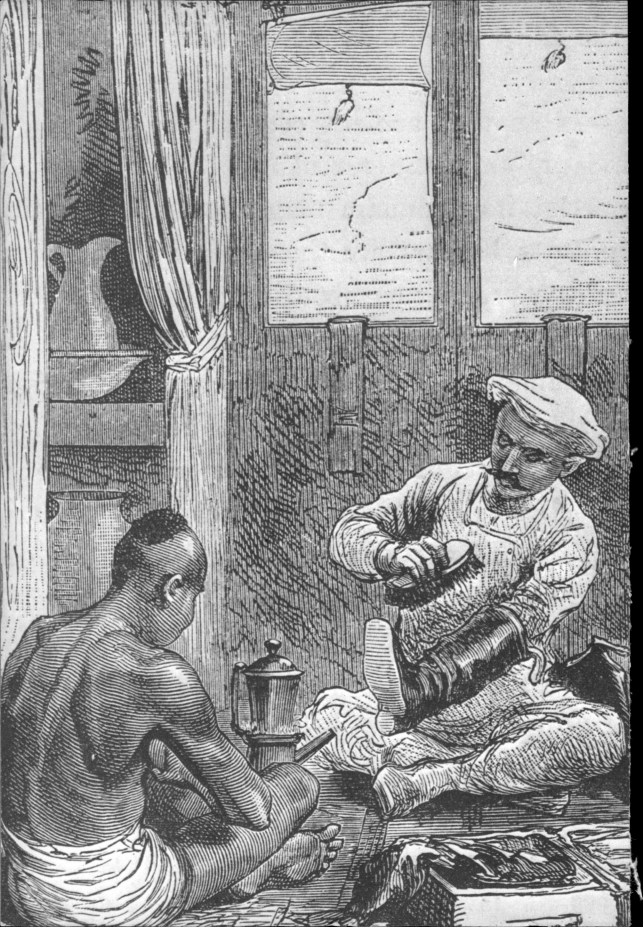